# Credit $mart
## Your Prescription to Healthy Credit in 60 Days or Less

First Published in 1996. Copyright © 2020 by: DAV Productions. All Rights Reserved. ISBN # 0-9721658-2-7

## DISCLAIMER

It is not the intention of the author of this work to provide legal, financial or advisory services. Our purpose is to inform, stimulate and guide you on the subject of responsible use and care o your credit. Therefore, we must specifically disclaim any risk, loss or liability, directly or indirectly, resulting from the use or application of any information contained in this book. The Reader Is Urged To Seek The Services Of An Attorney, Accountant Or Financial Advisor To Review And Analyze The Reader's Specific Situation.

## FEEDBACK

If you have any comments, suggestions or questions regarding this book, please email the author at iknowdoug@gmail.com

Publishing Consulting support provided by Agora Publishing www.AgoraPublishing.com

Editing and Formatting: Lyceum Editing, LyceumTestPrep@gmail.com

**Cover Illustration by Santhosh CHRiSTUDAS, Troll Cat Comics.**

I have been a professional freelance writer for 12 years and have written several books and hundreds of national magazine articles. It is evident that Doug knows exactly what he is talking about. The information, suggestions and techniques that he is making available to his students and to the readers of this book are obviously culled from years of experience and study on Doug's part, and would be helpful to anyone who deals in today's credit world (as we all do).

Steve O.
Professional Writer

I wanted to take this opportunity to let you know Doug that you are nothing short of a genius. Without your help my credit would have remained where it had been for so many years. . . down the drain! In fact, I had no idea what the status of my credit had been before you looked into each and every one of my credit reports. Not only did you take the time to explain each and every detail of the credit repair process to me, but you also went further. You showed me what to do once my credit has been repaired and how to follow up with many of the corrections you had made to my credit reports.

Dr. Michael C.
Chiropractor

Doug, for the last year Kelly and I worked very closely with you in order to improve her credit. Since she has now been able to obtain substantial credit lines and several mortgages, I felt it was important to write to you and express our appreciation. You are the first person we have met who talks straight. You say what you can and can't do. That is very important to us. You have been patient, up-front and we have had fun working with you. The other "credit specialists" we have met act like they own the moon and simply want to charge a fee and disappear.

John & Kelly R.
The Mentor Group

When we began working with Doug, I could barely talk about the subject without fighting back tears. Steven couldn't speak to creditors without losing his temper or making promises under pressure that we couldn't keep. So, we just stopped communicating with them all together. By the time Doug began working with us many of our debts had changed hands several times, interest was still compounding and there were so many collection letters that we filled a file drawer where we just threw them to accumulate. We had no idea who we owed and who was collecting! Doug has helped us remove incorrect, illegal data from our credit reports, negotiated us out of wage withholding and negotiated payments we can manage. It's worth it! It can be done! Doug Vairo can guide you through it!

Steve & Kate P.
Deacatur, GA

## About The Author

One of the most famous self-help books written during the past 50 years begins with the sentence '*Life is difficult.*' Three simple words, a short, declarative thought, yet, a concept that the vast majority of the folks who have peopled the face of this planet over the ages have found hard to accept as a 'neutral fact.' How patently unfair it seems to most of us, wrote Scott Peck, the author of *The Road Less Traveled*, that life is not only difficult, but is often a downright struggle.

Yet, he tellingly pointed out, the willing acceptance of life as a challenge is a trait that is found in all great men and women, and one of the hallmarks of a mature mind and a well-grounded spirit. Very few of those successful folks who hold this concept as one of the foundation blocks of their life philosophy have come upon it easily; it is not a lesson taught in books. Not only is life difficult, but also life can be a very harsh and often unforgiving teacher.

The triumph of mankind though, is that history's pages are filled with examples of men, women, peoples and nations whose successes were forged in the fires of adversity and shaped upon the anvil of struggle. And, simply put, the winners in the game of life were those who fully accepted the proposition that human existence is intrinsically difficult, and decided that the only realistic strategy was not to question why or pretend that universal laws should be otherwise, but to go out and meet life upon life's terms and persevere.

The wise folk of a hundred generations have all, in one fashion or another, reached the same conclusion; a joyful life is one that is lived facing problems and challenges square on, without quibble or question. Any other course of action leaves one in the land of shadowy doubt, fear and self-pity.

The book that follows is authored by one of life's winners. Doug Vairo was a born entrepreneur, and, beginning in 1974, dove headfirst into the business of building businesses. From successful commodity routes-he developed one of Tropicana's more extensive and profitable distribution networks-to a string of Hallmark card and gift shops, young Vairo learned how to build sizable enterprises over short periods of time.

Doug quickly grasped and mastered two of business' universal rules, number one that opportunity and adversity are often different faces of the same coin, i.e., the solution to someone's problem is often the basis of a good business proposition. The second rule was that of replication; build a good model, get the kinks out and go do it a dozen times over. Before he was 30, Doug was a business success story.

Deciding that he wanted to know how to appraise prospective business acquisitions in a more sophisticated manner, Doug attended Brooklyn College to study accounting. In his own words, he needed to 'know how to take a balance sheet apart in the same way a mechanic strips down a motor to find out what's going on with it, why it isn't working right. I wanted to be able to look at a troubled company find out right away if there was any hope of fixing it.' Eventually, his inherent need to constantly learn new disciplines lead him to acquire licenses as both an auctioneer and a real estate agent, and work successfully in both fields. Sitting at the top of his world and knowing that his winning business record could lead him to 'the big move, the real deal,' life for Doug Vairo was good.

Yet, in the flash of a few fleeting moments, or so it seemed to him at the time, Vairo's fortunes reversed, and a life that had been so bright and secure suddenly turned sour.

The first blow was the collapse of his marriage, and the resulting divorce filled his business dealings with a series of asset damaging wrangling matches that landed him in a weakened financial position. The second blow was crushing. As he began to pick up the pieces and move on, a serious and debilitating illness toppled Doug, leaving him bed-ridden for months, stripping him of his health, most of his income, and draining away his already diminished financial resources.

Emerging from his sick bed, Doug faced a bevy of business and personal creditors, whose very insistent ringing of his phone and the accompanying flurries of impolite and extremely demanding letters, put Doug into one of life's purest predicaments; flight or fight? Besides being blessed with an entrepreneurial streak, Doug quickly got that all-important life lesson cited above; Life is difficult. So? Get on with it.

Digging his heels in firmly, Vairo turned the tables on his creditors, seized the offensive and literally barraged *them* with phone calls and letters. After the initial shock of having the tables turned on them, most of his creditors agreed to work out payment plans with him that allowed Doug to begin to restore his credit immediately by having his credit reports marked '*paid as agreed*' on their accounts.

Creditors who refused to work with Doug and attempted to continue to use outlawed hardball collection tactics with him found that they'd grabbed a very legally savvy tiger by the tail. Doug not only had read and mastered the Fair Credit Reporting Act, the body of legislation that sharply curbed collection agencies harsh practices, but had devoured reams of articles from law journals around the country related to consumers successful forays against collectors using the legal powers of the act. His mastery of the law and the associated court decisions allowed Doug to go toe to toe with unscrupulous collection companies and walk away a winner.

As a born pursuer, collector and analyzer of knowledge, Doug now found a new calling. First on an informal basis, he began to shape his experience into notes to others he knew to be in the same predicament from which he just emerged. Soon he was authoring articles for local and then national print media, and before he realized it he had the manuscript for what was to become this book lying neatly typed before him. Partnering with the renowned and nationally syndicated radio personality and financial advisor Bruce Williams, Doug published the first edition of 'CREDIT SMART' to rave reviews and impressive sales.

Doug jokingly claims that he's only prouder of his other publication; a credit report that now boasts a FICO score of over 800 points, one of the highest credit ratings given by the reporting agencies and a testament to one man's decision to face life upon life's terms.

Doug's story does not end with the publication of this credit restoration program (it's far more than just a book so let's just call it what it is). A few years back he decided to enter and explore the Mortgage industry. Starting at an entry-level position, Doug rocketed to industry fame—he has the bank account and press clippings to prove it—by taking a local mortgage broker and turning it into a billion dollar company in little over two years. Mortgage bankers who had struggled their whole professional lives stood open mouthed and slack jawed as Doug streaked past them.

It has been our good fortune to become associated with Douglas Vairo. For Frank Langone, the Director of RETC Training, one of the nation's premier Real Estate and Mortgage Training Schools, to have someone of Vairo's experience and stature saunter through his doors one day expressing an urge 'pass some of what I've learned on to people,' has been as Frank describes it 'a surprising and truly inspiring pleasure.'

For myself, I stood in wonder as Doug took our small mortgage brokerage and rapidly grew it into a string of companies that have established a national presence, and have experienced financial success that was beyond my dreams, goals and comprehension.
I have also personally witnessed him intervene, time after time, in loan applications that are having trouble being approved due to the applicant's credit problems and quickly get them pointed in the right direction. It's truly an awesome and heartening experience to peer over his shoulder as he looks to 'just get things made right.'

In closing, my advice to those readers with damaged credit is to snatch this book up, read it cover to cover and 'plan your work and work your plan.' Before you know it your credit score will be sky high, surpassed only by the full measure of self-esteem you'll be enjoying as one of the special folks who decided to live life under life's terms and bravely face the daily challenge of being the proud occupant of a few precious square feet of this joyfully puzzling planet we call home.

Finally, to our professional associates in the Real Estate and Mortgage fields, take this book and change the lives of a few dozen people over the next couple of years for the better. It will be a highly profitable enterprise for you. Not only will you quickly develop a large network of folks who are returning to 'easy to finance' status, and who are grateful you got them there (i.e., loyal), but will also be able to immediately help lots of folks to cure credit blemishes, both the deserved and the undeserved, which will save deals and commissions for you.

Yet, as you sit counting your commissions, that warm, glowing feeling creeping over you won't be coming from your account balance, it'll be coming from your heart. What nobler enterprise could one be engaged in than aiding folks in the restoration of their family's security and well-being? Good health and prosperity to all.

                                                    **FXS**

## ACKNOWLEDGMENTS:

I would like to acknowledge with thanks the special contributions of Frank P. Langone of RETC TRAINING in editing, assembling, and compiling this work.

Douglas Vairo
Author

## <u>IMPORTANT AUTHOR NOTE</u>

PLEASE save the following website on your computer. If you learn nothing else from my book, you should SAVE this website. You will learn a TON of Credit information from this site. It should become your resource for ALL questions about credit.

# WWW.myFICO.COM

**Please feel free to email me directly at: iknowdoug@gmail.com**

# PREFACE

Not long after man crawled out of the caves, he discovered fi re. History demonstrates that ever since man found fi re, he has found a way to burn himself. Does that mean that fi re should be done away with?  Clearly not! We use fi re to heat our homes, cook our food and do all manner of very good things for us. But still, from time to time, people do burn their fingers and occasionally burn down their homes. In almost every instance, the fi re is not the demon, but rather the person who misused the match, the cigarette, or appliance to start the fi re.

So, the same it is true for credit. Credit in and of itself is neutral - it has no polarity - it is neither good nor bad. How it's used clearly can be for good or evil. Oftentimes people tell me, "I've solved my credit problems, I've cut up my credit cards." This is no solution. This is like taking all of your matches and putting them into a sink and soaking them. The matches in and of them- selves don't start evil fi res. Someone, carelessly or deliberately, must strike the match, which is simply a tool, and start that fi re. If putting the matches into the sink or cutting up the credit cards were the answer, then we could solve all of the murders that involved knives simply by destroying all knives. This is just another example of carrying what might appear to be a logical solution to a ridiculous conclusion. So, it is with credit.

Credit is a very useful tool, one that can serve us well. Consider a world without credit. We would all have to carry copious quantities of cash. Can you imagine going to a closing on a piece of real property where no mortgage is involved, with a wheelbarrow full of money? Obviously, ridiculous. A check, letter of credit, or some other negotiable instrument is far more convenient than the  wheelbarrow.

The same thing is true with other forms of credit. Notably credit cards.  It is much easier and more convenient to check into a hotel, rent a car, or make a retail purchase with "plastic" than it is to have a pocket full of money. Aside from the convenience, if a credit card is lost, your maximum exposure is $50.00. If you lose $20,000 in cash, your exposure is $20,000. On top of all this, while thieves do covet credit cards, it is seldom that they hold up some- one with a gun or a knife in order to relieve them of a credit card. But try walking down many streets with $20,000 in cash; if crooks know, you're dead meat!

The trick then is not cutting up credit cards if you have a problem, but rather learning how to control credit and make the credit your slave rather than your master. (No pun intended.) This little booklet is designed to help you first to understand what credit is all about, how it works, and give you solid information on how to use it to your advantage. It would be disingenuous not to recognize that there are some people who simply cannot control their use of credit, just as there are others whose first drink is an invitation to a drunken orgy or whose first bet is the first step to losing the family farm. For those relatively few people, cutting up the cards and having no credit whatsoever is probably the only viable solution. But for the rest of us, it is a matter of understanding what credit can and should do, and cannot and should not be expected to do, and use of a certain amount of that very difficult but necessary ingredient in our lives, "discipline".

It is in this context that the following information is offered. It is not meant to be a cure-all, and certainly not covering every facet of credit. Rather, it is a general overview as to how credit can serve you best. Like every other tool, once you master its use and its limitations, it will be a very useful tool - one that will serve you well.

No preface on this subject would be complete without a brief mention of those folks who have gotten themselves in over their heads through no fault of their own: unexpected medical bills, sometimes a spouse who has spent copious quantities of money without the knowledge or consent of the marital partner, or the loss of employment. There are many exceptions to those who are frivolously abusing their credit, but the result is the same. The solutions have to be determined. It is in this context and spirit that the authors hope that the information herein will be helpful to you.

# Table of Contents

Chapter 7:

# CHAPTER 1

## CREDIT CARDS IN GENERAL

WHY CREDIT CARDS ARE SO POPULAR
Credit cards are everywhere in our society today. It is almost impossible to transact many types of business in today's world without a credit card. These little pieces of plastic are so popular because we like speed and convenience. With credit cards, we can have the things we want when we want them.

For example, with a credit card you can pick up the telephone and order an item from an advertisement Within several days it is delivered to your door. You didn't have to leave the house, spend time looking for the merchandise, or use gasoline. You also didn't need to worry about whether you had enough money to pay for it.

Why are credit cards so popular? With a credit card, you can:

BUY NOW, PAY LATER. You can order any merchandise you want as long as you don't go over your credit limit, and then you can pay that borrowed amount back at the end of the month. Usually you have 28 days to pay that bill without charge. If you pay for your merchandise by check, many companies will wait weeks until it clears, because they have to worry about bounced checks. Your credit card order guarantees (unless you dispute the charge) that the bill will be paid; the seller gets its cash almost immediately. It's up to the issuer of the credit card – a bank or other company – to collect from you. That helps goods and services move faster.

CARRY LITTLE CASH. You can access your checking accounts or your credit lines at many banks throughout the United States and abroad if you need cash. You just punch the information into an automatic teller machine or go into any bank and request a certain amount of money. Should you lose your credit card, it's easy enough to make a telephone call and have the card canceled to prevent anyone else from using it and have it replaced almost immediately.

KEEP TRACK OF YOUR PURCHASES. Your monthly statement will tell you how much credit you have available, where your purchases were made, the date that the purchases were made, and many other important facts. In the future, credit cards may carry an embedded computer chip that will keep track of the same information.

Nowadays, some kinds of transactions almost require a credit card: Renting a car or reserving a hotel room can be difficult without one. For many people, they have become a virtual necessity.

## FOUR TYPES OF CREDIT CARDS

Let's talk about the types of credit cards now available:

1. Seller Credit Cards (also known as Store Charge Cards)

Seller credit cards are probably the oldest and most widely known form of credit card. They were issued by businesses years ago to help boost their sales and were usually issued to some of their better customers. They were customarily due and payable in full within 30 days. As time passed, the issuing businesses found that they were able to charge interest like the banks and extend their payment terms. Department stores, airlines, oil companies, and other major retailers issued cards exclusively for purchases of their own products or services: You can't use a JCPenney card to charge anything at Sears, for example. This serves a twofold purpose. First, it's a good marketing tool, because it makes customers feel that they're important people to that particular establishment and makes it easy for them to make purchases there. Second, the establishments can add to their profits by charging you interest. Many charge interest as high as 18 percent to 21.9 percent per year.

2. Bank Cards (such as MasterCard and Visa)

Bank cards were born in California. Four banks got together and decided to issue a single card that became known as the MasterCharge. Today, this card is known as MasterCard. These banks decided they would honor the sales slips of any merchant participating in the program, and that's pretty much how the system works today. Each bank that issues a MasterCard or Visa agrees to accept the sales slips of all the merchants who are members of that particular MasterCard or Visa plan. This makes it possible for consumers to go out and buy any products or services throughout the United States and even abroad without paying cash or writing a check. At the end of each month, the consumers get bills detailing what charges they made. The extended payment plan makes it convenient for people to budget if they want to buy a big-ticket item such as a refrigerator or television. For example, if you want to buy a $2,000 item, yet you don't want to wait six months or a year while you save up for it (during which time the price might go up), you can use your bank card to buy the item right away. When you get your bill, instead of making the total $2,000 payment, you may choose to pay $50 a month including interest charges. Part will go toward interest; part will go toward principal. In recent years, banks have earned anywhere from 10 percent interest on preferred customers' accounts to as much as 23 percent interest on others. One important thing to keep in mind is that MasterCard and Visa do not actually issue you the credit. These organizations are clearing houses for the banks or others that issue the credit cards. For example, when you get a credit card from a bank, the name of that institution will be on your credit card, and it deter- mines your credit limit based on its own lending criteria. In some cases, this bank may be only a sales agent for a larger bank, with which you will have to deal if you have a problem.

3. Travel and Entertainment Cards (such as American Express or Diners Club)

These usually go by the name "T & E Cards." American Express, Diners Club, Carte Blanche, and other cards of that nature are all T & E cards, or charge cards. The major difference between charge cards and credit cards is that credit cards usually offer revolving terms, so you don't have to pay the total amount at the end of each month, whereas you do with charge cards. This means that at the end of each month the total amount that you have charged is due and payable in full. Only recently have some of these cards been changing their policies because they realize that a lot of people don't want to pay their bills in full at the end of the month; they want more flexibility. For example, the American Express Green Card had a plan letting you charge airline tickets and extend the payments over 12 months, but that was the only type of charge that could be extended. It now has a program with its Optima Card that allows you to pay off the balance on a revolving-type minimum payment basis – the same as a credit card. American Express also has a card called the Gold Card, which has a dual function. It works the same as the basic Green Card. You can pay it off in full or, if you like, you can sign your name when the bill comes. By signing your name you activate your line of credit. The credit line is extended by a lending institution named on the card. When you use your credit line you must deal with the lending institution and not American Express. You will have a separate agreement with that lending institution. With its Optima Card, which is one of its premier cards, you can go to an automatic teller machine and use your personal identification number to obtain cash up to your credit limit. At this writing, the only limitation on the Optima Card is that it will allow you to take out only up to $500 in any seven-day period, whereas most bank credit cards allow you to withdraw your entire limit in one transaction. However, some cards limit cash advances to $300 or $500, even though you might have a $5,000 or

$10,000 limit. With basic American Express cards, there is no set spending limit but, as we said, you have to pay off the entire amount each month. That's the major difference between the travel and entertainment cards and your bank and seller credit cards.


4. Debit Cards

Debit cards differ from bank cards and T & E cards in that they do not enable you to borrow any money, not even briefly. With charge cards and credit cards, you have a float period of, say, 28 days before your bill comes.

However, your debit card automatically removes money from your checking account. If you go into a store and use your debit card to buy a $400 item, and you have $1,000 in your checking account, your checking account is automatically reduced by that $400 to $600. It's like writing a check.

## PREFERRED, GOLD, PLATINUM, SECURED, AND UNSECURED CARDS

### P referred Cards

Preferred credit cards are usually offered to a financial institution's best customers. These are people who either have high incomes or have been with the bank for many years and have always paid their bills on time. The bank feels sure that these people are capable of handling their credit in any type of situation and, of course, the bank is very happy to be earning interest by raising the credit limit of longtime customers who have proven their credit-worthiness. The bank is obviously making money lending money, and it is minimizing its risk by lending to these preferred customers. Usually when you first apply for credit or don't earn a substantial amount of money, these preferred cards are not easy to obtain: They usually take time. From a consumer's point of view, preferred credit cards are just that – they're preferred because they carry a preferred or low interest rate. For example, if the interest rate on most cards is 17 percent and 18 percent, a preferred customer will pay only 10 percent or 12 percent. The interest a lending institution charges is in direct relation to the amount of risk it incurs, and preferred customers have proved themselves to be excellent (i.e. low risk borrowers) risks.

### Gold Cards

"Gold" cards are now offered by major credit card companies. Probably the most prominent gold card issued today is the American Express Gold Card. Usually these gold cards, which are similar to the preferred cards, have a minimum credit limit of $5,000. The reason for the gold is its prestige. It's flashy and it shows that you're a more valued customer. However, it does not necessarily have a preferred interest rate like the preferred card. It just means that it carries a higher credit limit.

## Platinum Cards

The third type of card – the "Platinum" card – is issued by American Express and has an almost unlimited credit ceiling. This is only for the most elite customers whom the banks trust to borrow substantial amounts of money on such a card. This is a card the average person doesn't really have much use for, so we won't go into much detail with it. You cannot apply for a "Platinum" card. You must be "invited" to apply, and you must have spent over $10,000 on a Gold card for two or more consecutive years.

## Secured Credit Cards

A secured credit card is just what it says: It is secured by collateral, a cash deposit. People who do not have credit or have had bad credit in the past and want to re-establish credit have very few options other than using secured credit cards. To get a secured credit card, you must go to a bank that issues secured credit cards – not all banks do – and open a savings account. The minimum deposit is usually $300. The bank then issues you a MasterCard or Visa secured by your savings account. Some banks will give you a 100 percent credit line against your account and others will allow only 50 percent to 80 percent of your deposit. In many cases, you won't be able to withdraw any amount from your savings account while you have that MasterCard or Visa. After the first year, the bank will have a payment history on you and may be willing to release some or all of your security deposit if your history has been good.

## Unsecured Credit Cards

An unsecured credit card is just that: unsecured. The lending institution has no security or collateral if you default on the loan. In other words, if you have a $2,000 line of credit and for some reason fail to pay, the bank really has no specific collateral that it can attach to satisfy that $2,000 debt. It will come after any and all assets it can get. Unsecured credit cards are more prevalent today because the banks rely heavily on credit information from credit reporting agencies and the person's credit history. Besides, on amounts less than $5,000 it is too expensive for banks to sell your collateral.

## How to Establish Credit

One way to establish credit is to try to obtain some of the simpler forms of credit cards, such as oil company credit cards and cards at some of the major department stores. They will usually issue you a card with a small credit limit, but if you can establish a good repayment history over the next nine months to a year by paying as agreed, you will establish a good credit rating.

Another way to establish credit is by using a secured credit card, which is a fast way of getting credit.

## Instant Credit

Many merchants, such as department stores, jewelry stores, and tire stores, will immediately give you a temporary credit card to use in the store the day you go there, as long as you already have a MasterCard, Visa, or American Express card.

The reasoning is that if you're credit-worthy enough to have one or more of these cards, then you must be credit-worthy enough for this store, too. In many cases, they'll issue you a credit limit of several hundred dollars to use that day, and then, after they check your credit file and your history, either they will issue you a permanent card, quite possibly with a higher limit, or they will yank your card if they don't like what they find out.

That's one way of getting instant credit and not tying up your other credit lines. You have more flexibility to pay these bills as you see fit within your own budget.

Within the last several years, many merchants have been advertising "buy now, no interest charge, and no payments for several months." These offers usually come out late in the year because the merchants want to clear out their old stock. They know a lot of people are spending money on Christmas shopping, and they want these buyers to come in and spend their money with them. They have found that the best way to do that is to extend payments until March or April. Sometimes finance charges will accrue from the date of the purchase, if not paid in full on the agreed-upon date, and sometimes they won't. It's all a matter of how the seller wants to attract consumers' attention. This is another means of getting instant credit. In many cases, they won't even check your credit if the purchase is under several thousand dollars.

Used car dealerships often offer such packages to the consumer. They use the automobiles they sell as collateral. It's a "buy here/pay here" transaction. This is another way of establishing a good credit rating. Go to a used car dealership and buy a car for several thousand dollars. Make payments on time and have the dealer send the information in to the credit bureau. Anything positive like this that you can add to your credit report will greatly enhance your credit history.

Increasing Your Credit Line

A good way to increase your credit line is to wait approximately six to nine months after you obtain your first credit cards, then re-apply for higher credit limits with those same banks.

Many of the banks have a more positive attitude toward customers who have proved themselves with a good track record over the past six to nine months, and they want to keep them as customers. They also feel that they've made money with them in the past, so they will increase their credit lines. Sometimes they'll increase a credit line by 10 percent and sometimes by as much as 100 per- cent. Some of the banks will ask the customers to fill out complete applications like the original forms that they sent in. Other banks have simpler forms that just ask by how much you would like to increase your credit line.

You can even call on the telephone and have your lines increased. In many cases, the operator can make the decision right then by looking at your credit history. Sometimes, if it's just emergency cash that you need, or you want to purchase a large-ticket item, you merely need to explain what you intend to do with the credit line increase, and the operator will increase it enough to cover that purchase.

It's often just as easy to write a letter, giving your account number and asking the institution to check your credit again if you're asking for a large enough increase. Sometimes you may want to indicate the specific amount of increase that you want. Other times it's more to your advantage to leave that amount open to the banks.

On the application, one card company asked what credit limit was desired and the applicant wrote down $10,000. The company replied, declining to give the $10,000. A little bit further on in the letter declining the $10,000 limit, the company stated that it was declining only the requested limit. It was willing to issue a credit line of $5,000 and if that was satisfactory, nothing needed to be done – it would send the card. If a larger credit line was needed, the applicant would have to contact the company again. The applicant decided to do nothing and took the $5,000. Sometime later the card came in the mail.

Some banks increase credit lines automatically every six months to a year. Other banks will not increase customers' credit lines unless they specifically ask to have their lines increased. You'll need to find out from your bank what their criteria are for increasing the credit ceiling.

Another good option – though this is a lot more limited than using credit cards – is using an overdraft account in connection with your checking account. This is an automatic loan that kicks in if you are overdrawn. You pay only if you "borrow" the money and only for the time you have it.

Interest Expense and Finance Charge Calculation

There are three popular credit card finance charge calculation methods. It's important for you to understand which method your banks use, as well as the relative benefits or disadvantages of each.

Previous Balance Method

The finance charge is computed on the entire amount of balance due. It does not take into consideration any payments made until the following month.

Adjusted Balance Method

The bank computes a finance charge against the remaining balance at the end of that particular billing period. Interest on purchases made during the month is not calculated into the amount until the end of the next billing period. This is one of the least expensive methods for the card holder.

Ave rage Daily Balance Method

This is by far the most common method in use today. Calculations are made by taking your previous balance and subtracting any payments received. Your finance charge is computed on the amount left over. Before you apply for any of these cards, you may want to ask the banks to send you a copy of their billing rights. One word of caution: Make sure you read the entire billing rights. The billing rights will tell you exactly what method is used, how much is charged as an annual membership fee, what the interest rate is and, most important if you plan to use your cards for cash advances, exactly how much the cash advance fees are. Some cards charge 65 cents per transaction and allow you to withdraw the entire amount of your available credit limit in one transaction. For example, if you have a $5,000 card with $3,000 unused credit, you can go into a bank and borrow the $3,000 in cash and you'll be charged only a 65 cent trans- action fee. Some of the other banks will charge you "points." Some banks will charge you 2 percent of whatever amount you borrow. For example, if you went to a bank and borrowed $2,000, you would be charged 2 per- cent, which would be $40. If you don't read your billing rights before you make these transactions, you could be in line for a rude awakening. Some banks will also charge you a cash advance fee of $1 or $2, or even as much as $5 or $6 on top of the 2 percent. Plus, they're going to charge you interest on the total amount that's extended to you. Therefore, if you borrow $2,000, they'll charge you 2 percent, which they'll put in your credit card statement, plus your cash advance fee, which let's say in this case is anoth- er $5. That means you borrowed $2,000, yet what they have on your state- ment as a cash advance against your line (including these fees) is $2,045. And they'll begin charging you interest on that total amount, so you're actually paying interest on the cash advance fees and the 2 percent fee that you paid as points. Make sure that you read all your statements through carefully so that you know exactly what your credit rights are with each individual company.

Obtaining Cards When You Are Self-Employed

We may consider some things minor and overlook them. Banks don't. You have to remember that you're dealing with banks and institutions that set their own rules, and they have to be conservative because they're using depositors' money. They have to protect that money. They need to try to figure out who the most worthy applicants are. They're not going to lend money to just anyone. They're not going to lend money to people just because they say they need the money because they're down and out. They want to make sure that the borrower is going to be able to repay the loan.

Usually, they find that the best risks are professional people, such as doctors and lawyers, as well as people who have been in the same job for a long time. Instability can hurt you. So, can being self-employed.

Self-employment is great from an entrepreneurial standpoint: You're out on your own, relying on yourself and making your own decisions. But from the banks' viewpoint, you are a risk: A high percentage of all new enterprises go out of business the first year, and quite a few more go out of business the second year. Therefore, you need to have a long, stable track record in a particular business to make the bank feel comfortable.

There are several ways to make the bank feel more comfortable about your self-employment. One of those ways is to have your company incorporated and name yourself the president or the vice president rather than the owner. Pay yourself a salary so you can make a W-2 form for yourself. If you need further information on how to do this, seek the advice of a competent accountant.

Whether you send in your tax returns if they ask for them is up to you. It depends on how badly you need the credit. Why would they ask? The reasoning is that no one reports more income on a tax return than they actually made. Many, of course, say they earned less. Also, if you don't have W-2 paystubs to prove your income, tax returns will be needed.


P re-Approved Credit Cards

Pre-approved credit cards are not exactly what they advertise themselves to be. Folks receive applications for pre-approved credit cards and assume that they are already approved for the line of credit. This is not the way it works. What really happens is that the credit card company or the bank that issues the "pre-approved" credit card buys a mailing list from a credit bureau or some other source. They buy the names of people who have a good credit rating and a sufficient income level within a specific geographical area. The company sets whatever criteria it wishes. The bank then sends what appears to be applications for pre-approved cards with pre-approved lines of credit to these names.

When a bank sends you one of these, it shows up on your credit report as an inquiry. However, it does not tell you what bank made the inquiry. That's all encoded information. What it says is "PRM," followed by a number. (PRM stands for promotion.) Usually a promotion will stay on your credit report for six months.

Once they send you this pre-approved credit card application, they often ask you just to sign it and fill in a little further information like address, amount of income and a couple of other simple items. Banks differ on the amount of information they request for a pre-approved card. At this point you'll sign the bottom of the pre-approved statement and send it back to the bank, which will evaluate your credit history thoroughly by obtaining your credit report from the credit bureau. That will also show up as an inquiry, but this time it will show the exact name of the bank. For example, if it's First National Bank, it will show up as a promotion and then maybe a month later when you send your application back it will show up as "First National Bank."

This means you'll have two inquiries from the same bank. You might want to write back to the bank and say, "Listen, if you're going to check my credit again, please remove the promotion from my credit report." Sometimes they'll readily comply and sometimes they won't. Many bankers do understand that's all they are. However, they still can show up as excessive inquiries, or so many inquiries within a six-month or one-year period, and you don't want excessive inquiries on your credit report.

Once they check your credit, guess what? They might deny you a card based on any of a number of factors: too many inquiries, excessive credit obligations, income that does not meet the required level, or whatever reason they have that would prevent them from issuing you a card.

Once that happened to me, so I wrote a letter that was businesslike – no abusive language, no threats or anything like that. You always want to be nice and understanding because you get more with honey than you do with vinegar. (That theme will be repeated throughout this book.) Always act as if you're not in a rush. Have the attitude that there's a minor problem you need to work out, you don't understand why something was done, and you'd like them to explain it to you.

I explained briefly that I thought a pre-approved card meant that it was already approved. What else would pre-approval mean? I explained that if it wasn't already approved, I didn't appreciate them sending it indicating that it was. I went on to say that I had a good credit standing and they must have gotten my name from a credit bureau or some other institution which showed that I had reasonable credit. After I sent my letter, I was issued a card.

Just remember, when you get something in the mail that indicates you are pre-approved and afterwards they decline your application, find out what the reasons are and then write a direct, courteous letter. You are entitled to an explanation.

You need to put your best foot forward when you're dealing with bankers and creditors. Make a good impression. Most people will not take time to write back to companies. They'll just let everything slide. Take the time to question and challenge any declines you receive.


Beware of Offers Like This!

"Wait a minute!" you might say. "I don't have to go through all this credit fix-up baloney. I can get a gold card with up to $2,500 instant credit even though I have no credit, bad credit, or even if I declared bankruptcy. It says so on an advertisement I saw."

I have only two words to say: "Caveat emptor!" This is Latin for "Let the buyer beware!" You must read the fine print. What you are getting is a catalog charge card. You use your "credit" to purchase merchandise at full retail price from the company issuing the card. You may pay up to five times the competitive price. You cannot take cash advances or purchase items anywhere else. After a year of use, the company promises to help you obtain a MasterCard or Visa. Bull!

How can they give you credit with no credit check or collateral? Easy.

They require that you give them a down payment on all the merchandise you buy. Guess what? The amount they require covers the cost of the item, and they give you credit for the rest. For example, if an item sells for $100, and it cost them $10, they would ask you for a down payment of $20 and finance the rest. How nice of them to let you charge the remaining balance, even after they have made their profit on your down payment!

This is not a good way to establish credit or purchase merchandise. In short, forget it!

# CHAPTER 2

## BANKS

═══════════════════════════════════════

═══════════════════════════════════════

Selecting Your Banks by Knowing What to Look For

Before applying to any bank, you will want to ask some questions to make sure it fits your situation. Some of these banks will tell you that there are no annual fees, but on the back of their statements they will reveal that they'll charge you 2 percent for cash advances and hit you with all kinds of other fees. That's why you need to check into several banks.

One mistake is not finding out exactly what their terms and conditions are before application. If you find that you get a card and you have not read the terms, don't worry. Many of these banks will allow you to read the terms before you make a charge, and if you're not satisfied with them, you simply cut the card up and send it back to the company. In many cases, the terms of an agreement will indicate, "By using this card, you have accepted the terms and conditions that we have listed." In other words, if you don't read the terms and conditions and you use the card, you're bound by whatever it states. Ignorance is no excuse, so be sure to read the terms and conditions so you know exactly what your rights are and how the issuing card company handles its accounts.

## The following are several questions you may want to ask:

1. What do you charge for a cash advance?

2. What is the maximum cash advance I can take on my card in any one day?
    Some banks limit their cash advances to $500 within any seven-day

period. Others allow only a total of $300 or $400, even though your credit line might be $4,000 or $5,000.

3. How often does your bank review for credit-line increases?

Some banks will review every three months; some six months; some every year.

4. What cards do you issue, and what are the limits that you issue?

Make sure that they're specific on this. Many banks will issue both a MasterCard and a Visa and split the limit between them. For example, instead of getting one card for a $2,000 limit, you'll get one MasterCard for $1,000 and one Visa for $1,000. They're actually the same account, so every time you charge on either card, it goes on the same account. What's the sense in having both cards? It just adds to the number of cards that you have and makes it a little harder to keep track of all of them. So, if they say that they issue both cards on the same account, request one or the other, and tell them that you want the entire credit line to be issued on that particular card. In the future, you may be able to apply for the other card and have a separate line of credit with that card.

5. What credit reporting agency do you use?

They'll usually tell you which credit agency they use. Write on your application that that is the only credit reporting agency you wish them to contact. Most of the time these banks will check only one credit report. It's usually the one that is local to your area. Sometimes they'll check several of them, but that's usually on larger loans. It doesn't hurt to write, "Please use this specific credit reporting agency."

6. What is your annual fee?

Some banks charge $10 and others charge as much as $40. Some companies don't charge any annual fee, but that's now becoming the exception rather than the rule unless you ask. When asked, many will waive the fee.

7. What interest rate do you charge and how do you calculate it?

8. Do I have to have a bank account with you to get a Visa or a MasterCard?

 If that's necessary, then it's just a secured credit card.

 These are important questions, but you don't have to ask all of them. Just ask, "Would you please send me the terms and conditions of your credit card?" Then you can read through the credit terms and get full, accurate answers to all the questions just listed. In fact, you will find answers to questions you might not even think of asking.

Savings & Loans' MasterCards and Visas

 Savings and loans that offer secured cards, whether nationwide or statewide, tend to practice a more lenient lending policy. The deposit required to secure a MasterCard or Visa will range from as little as $100 to as much as $2,500, and your credit line may vary from 50 percent to 150 percent of your deposit, depending on where you apply. Essentially, you set your own credit limits.

 A number of savings and loans also offer a debit card. A debit card is tied to your checking account with that particular savings and loan, and each transaction is debited from your checking account at the time of the transaction.

# CHAPTER 3

## OBTAINING CREDIT

THE MECHANICS OF CREDIT SCORING

Different institutions use different scoring criteria. We doubt that you will discover the exact system any lending institution uses, but if you ask, that lender will more than likely let you know what area you are deficient in. Depending on the criteria, different institutions have different point totals for passing. That difference can be important to you: A loan that four banks in a row refuse may be approved by the fifth – or the sixth.

In general, here are the items banks may use to score your credit:

➢ Age. In general, people in their prime earning years – mid-20s to mid-60s score the highest.

➢ Marital status. In general, married people do better than those who are single, divorced or widowed.

➢ Dependents. Too many dependents past a certain point can be a liability.

➢ Years with present employer. The more, the better.

➢ Type of occupation. Professionals often score the highest, and skilled workers score higher than unskilled workers.

➢ Total monthly income.

➢ Monthly liabilities (bills, payments on other debts). The less, the better.

➢ Type of residence. Owners are preferred over renters.

➢ Years at present address.

➢ Years at previous address.

➢    Home telephone. It should be listed in your name.

➢    Savings and checking accounts.

➢    Previous loans.

For more information on credit scoring, refer to the sample section at the end of this chapter. In recent years banks and other lending institutions have narrowed their guidelines. They are no longer allowed to base their scoring decisions on things like age, race, religion etc.

## Preparing One Application to Use as a Clone

For your own records, fill out one application that includes all the information that might be needed; it will serve as a "template" for all future applications. Inconsistencies can cause problems, because the banks to which you apply may report your answers, which can show up on your credit file.

Be consistent about using the information from your template. Of course, your circumstances can change. If you start making more money, report that: It will work to your advantage. If you move, show your new address. Overall, however, it's best to report the same information to everyone.

## Understanding the Loan Officer's Perspective

When loan officers review your application, they take many factors into consideration. Among the major points are neatness and the legibility of your application.

An application filled out in pencil, crayon, or any kind of ink that runs or smears, or any other messiness, will make a bad first impression, because it will make you look rushed or careless. A bad first impression can continue to color the entire business relationship.

# HERE ARE SOME OTHER THINGS LOAN OFFICERS CHECK:

Established checking or savings accounts. They like to see accounts held a long time, and they especially like to see accounts in their own banks.

Your track record on previous loans. That's usually established by checking your credit. They look to see if you've had bad credit in the past and if you've tried to straighten it out. Many bank loan officers, if they see that you had some financial trouble in the past but have added consumer statements and have sincerely tried to work it out, will consider you a better risk. Sometimes the fact that you came through a bad time will even show up as a positive. On your applications, don't be afraid to tell them that you have had a rough time. Add consumer statements to your credit file, so they will show a consistency between your application and your credit file.

Home ownership. Home ownership shows that you are more stable and you're not readily going to leave the area.

Employment record. Bankers like to make sure that you're stable and you're not jumping around from job to job. Of course, if you have done so in the same industry for advancement, you might want to make note of that on a separate sheet of paper with your application and explain anything that might seem negative or out of the ordinary. That will make the loan officer feel more comfortable and at ease.

In general, you should be upfront with loan officers, especially about factors that might appear to detract from your creditworthiness. It's better to explain those negatives in advance than to force the loan officers to ask; sometimes they won't and you will lose points.

If you ensure that they know the reasons for anything that may appear negative or out of the ordinary, they will feel better. Little extra steps like making a good first impression and explaining anything out of the ordinary can change a rejection into an approval.

## What Banks Don't Like to See on Credit Applications

Here are a few examples of entries a bank loan officer may not like to see on an application:

➢ New businesses (new businesses go out of business at an alarming rate).

➢ Unskilled labor as a source of income.

➢ Hotels or boarding homes as residential addresses.

➢ Frequent changes in employment.

➢ Frequent changes in address.

➢ High debt-to-income ratio.

➢ Criminal record

➢ Bankruptcies.

➢ Self-employed status, especially when the applicant is working out of the home.

➢ No telephone number.

Bank Loans

Applying for and obtaining a bank loan is really not all that difficult. If you are well-prepared when you go to the bank, look neat, speak calmly, and don't seem to be in a rush for a loan or to need the money for some crazy reason, you stand a good chance of putting the loan officer in a positive mood. If you can make a good first impression (and we have some tips on that later in this chapter) and your record shows you are a good credit risk, you should have no trouble obtaining your loan – even if your loan seems to go a little higher than your debt-to-income ratio should be.

Borrowing over your ratio strictly for a personal loan is not a good idea. However, if it's for a business loan, and you really think you're going to make it, you can sometimes get the loan by being persistent. Be honest with yourself about your chances of repaying the loan based on your proposed business. If you're not honest, you're going to get yourself into a bad situation.

Credit can help you or harm you. It can help you leverage your way into financial success – or it can impoverish you, ruining your credit report, miring you in debt, and bringing you lawsuits. Be very confident that you're going to be able to pay back any loans you apply for.

Credit is not a game. It's a very serious business. Be honest on your applications. If you're not, banks can sue you or even press charges for fraud.

Bear in mind that a bank is in the rental business, just like an apartment landlord or a videotape store. Taking out a loan is renting the bank's money, and the interest you pay is the rent. The bank's profit comes out of that interest.

Don't feel bad about paying interest. Like your business, the bank is entitled to make a profit, and interest is how banks make theirs. You need to calculate the interest you pay into the cost of your goods or whatever services that you're going to be providing with those funds.

## The Six C's of Credit

Most people who teach about credit use the "three C's of credit." They are: capacity, collateral and character. We like to use six C's because three C's are for the bank, and the other three are for the consumer.

The consumer's three C's are being cool, calm, and collected.

Of course, you have control over all six, but being cool, calm, and collected will help you to make better decisions, especially if you're having an in-person interview. It will show the banker that you have more control over yourself and that you're a conservative type, which is what the banks like to see. Demonstrating that you have good character and you're a cool, calm, and collected person will often be enough to throw a questionable loan, or a loan that's marginal, into your favor.

A number-crunching bank strictly goes by the numbers, period. It's a little more difficult to obtain a loan if your debt-to-income ratio is not in line with what the bank expects unless you're a very, very good customer of that bank.

A people bank would be more likely to extend credit, especially if it's a smaller bank – a community bank that's locally owned and operated. That kind of bank is becoming more and more rare as the little banks are being gobbled up.

The three C's for banks are:

## Capacity

Capacity means: "Will the borrower have enough income on a fairly steady basis to pay off this loan amount? Can he afford the monthly payments that he is incurring, plus whatever monthly payments he already has out-standing?" Since most people don't buy large ticket items with cash, they need to show that they have enough money coming in over a long period of time to pay off their debts. Of course, one of the measures that bankers use is the debt-to-income ratio, and each bank has a little different ratio.

## Collateral/Capital

Simply, these are items that you, the borrower, can pledge as security. If you default on your loan, the bank has the right to take your collateral as payment. The bank will sell your collateral, and if it doesn't cover the total amount owed, the bank can file a deficiency judgement against you. Collateral makes the bank feel more comfortable, especially if it can get more than the loan amount.

## Character/Credibility

Your character, believe it or not, is a very important factor in the determination of whether to lend you money. Since the likelihood of your knowing a banker personally is slim, there are several ways that you can show a lender that you are of good character. One way is to have a good credit report. Since the banker doesn't know you, he has to rely on what other lenders say about your past. That's one reason why it is important to have a clean credit report. If you had problems in the past, you should be honest about them. This will indicate that you're of good character and that you do not run away from your responsibilities. A second method is excellent letters of recommendation. You may need to ask a few businessmen you know to write you a letter of recommendation. We have included sample letters at the end of this chapter.

The three C's for you are:

## Cool

This means that you should be controlled. Don't be nervous. That's not easy. You may need to practice. Being cool means not having sweaty palms. Relax, the worst he can do is say no.

## Calm

According to Webster's Dictionary, "calm" means "not excited or agitated; nearly or completely motionless." That doesn't mean you should be like a statue. It just means don't act fidgety like Rodney Dangerfield.

## Collected

To be collected is to be self-possessed (that doesn't mean being possessed by the devil). It means being composed and having your thoughts collected. Try not to ad lib. Have all your information collected in an organized and readable fashion. Don't be glib.

## The Interview

Take some care before the interview to make the best possible impression:

## Dress the part.

When you go into the bank, don't go dressed in work clothes and work boots. If you're in a business that gets you dirty, change your clothes and clean up. Make sure you look your best. It's important to make a very good first impression because you don't get a second chance to create a first impression. You could be the nicest, most trustworthy person in the world and have the best character. But if a loan officer looks at you and you look like a homeless panhandler, you're dead meat. That's exactly what many people do when they go into banks: They look like deadbeats. The loan officer is going to get a negative first impression of you. If you have an extremely good financial statement, you can be thought of as eccentric. But if you need that bank officer more than he needs you, you need to play the game. You might say, play by the rules. Remember the Golden Rule: "He who has the gold makes the rules."

You just want to make sure your objective is met, which is obtaining the loan. If you went on a golf course and you were teeing off on a hole that was 300 yards away, you wouldn't take out your putter to hit off the tee. You would take out your 1-wood to drive the ball down the fairway (well, maybe), because that's the proper way to do it. So, when you go in for a bank loan, do it the proper way. Sometimes it feels a little embarrassing to be dressed up in a suit and a tie when you're not used to wearing suits. Call it a monkey suit or whatever you want to call it, but that's one of the tools of the trade if you're going to go directly into a bank and borrow funds. You should, however, look comfortable.

It doesn't really matter if, for example, you clean septic tanks for a living. If you're making a good living at it, you've been doing it for several years, you show stability and you've got a good income flow, the loan officer is going to feel good about your ability to repay. It's a stable industry and if you go in there dressed in a suit and tie, with clean fingernails and a neat haircut, and you present yourself in a very positive manner, the banker is going to see that you took the extra effort and that you're concerned about yourself. He'll figure that you're also going to be concerned about him and the bank's money; that's a positive for you. It's just another "plus" to add to obtaining a loan. You wouldn't fill out an application with crayons or in pencil. Dressing neatly is just one of those things that give you a positive image.

Bring any documents you might want.

There is no harm in bringing one of your credit reports to the initial meeting with a loan officer. Just remember that across the face of your credit reports it will say "Consumer Copy Only" or something of that nature. Banks and lending institutions prefer to receive these reports directly from the credit bureau for complete accuracy; after all, an applicant might alter the report.

However, you may want to bring the report with you to get an indication of how likely the loan approval will be. If you can work it out so that they will tell you, "Yes, we'll give you a loan if this information checks out," then ask the bank to run a credit check. On the other hand, the information on the report may indicate a problem, and you can ask if that problem can be straightened out.

Be persistent.

Winston Churchill said, "Never, never, never give up!" Success is 90 percent perspiration and 10 percent inspiration. It has been said, "Persistence is 90 percent of anything that you do." It's true! More people succeed by being persistent than they do by being knowledgeable. There are a lot of people out there who have all the knowledge in the world and have been to all kinds of universities and colleges, but they're stocking shelves at a convenience store. There are also many people who don't even have a high school diploma and are millionaires. Why? Because they never gave up.

Keep on trying, because if you give up then you'll never know what could have been. At least if you make a strong effort and keep on trying you're going to know. People will respect you more and you will respect yourself more if you keep trying. We've been turned down several times when looking for loans, but we never gave up and finally found the needed capital. After that, those banks that originally wouldn't lend us the funds started to solicit our business. Then it was our turn to turn them down.

Try for an unsecured loan.

When you're applying for these loans, whether you're applying for a credit card or a personal loan for a vacation or anything of that nature (aside from capital improvements such as home remodeling or durable goods, such as a refrigerator), try to get an unsecured loan. That gives you more flexibility in case adverse situations come along and you need to work out a new repayment schedule.

"Unsecured" means that the bank can't repossess anything specific because you did not use specific collateral: It has to come after you as a whole. Collecting such a debt can be difficult; it is often turned over to a collection agency, which at best will garner the bank only a portion of the amount owed.

If someone who defaults has used his possessions as collateral, the bank has the right to liquidate those items and apply that money against whatever amount is outstanding.

For example, let's say you owe the bank $10,000 and used your house furnishings and your automobile as collateral. If you defaulted on the loan, the bank would be able to take those items from you and sell them. Let's say they bring in $8,000; you have lost them, and you still owe the bank $2,000.

On the other hand, if it was an unsecured loan and you wanted to work something out with the bank to repay it, the bank would normally be willing to make some sort of arrangement with you. For example, if you sold your fancy automobile and got $6,000, but you still needed transportation for yourself so you bought a cheap car for $1,000, you would be able to give the bank $5,000 and thereby satisfy a large portion of the outstanding balance. You would maintain more control over your own finances and over your own life.

Giving up control to other people can be dangerous, because you don't know from day to day what's going to happen. It's the same thing as working for someone. You don't know if you're going to walk in that door one day and the boss is going to lay you off because things are going bad or because he doesn't like the way you look anymore, or he thinks you're making too much money in the company. You don't have the flexibility that you do when you're self-employed.

Keep your finances in such a way that you're in control.

Take your time in answering questions.

Do not volunteer any extra information other than what the banker asks you. We're not telling you to be misleading or to hide any facts. We're just telling you to answer only the questions relevant to obtaining the loan. If you start running off at the mouth about different things, the banker is going to pick up on a lot of gratuitous information, and if the information doesn't fit together it can be negative. The banker may feel that you're telling him a story just to get his money, and that you're going to run away with the cash.

Whenever the banker asks you a question, don't feel embarrassed about taking your time. It indicates that you are thinking that you're being conservative about it, and that you're weighing all the options.

Bankers are trained to think of the worst scenario. They always think: "What is the worst possible thing that could happen and what will happen to my money if that happens. Is there collateral to cover my risk?" You need to think like a banker so that you can overcome their objections.

If you think people don't run off with the money, you are definitely mistaken. More loans go bad than you would think. You don't realize it because the banks are obviously not going to advertise that so many loans are going bad. Outside legal ads, they don't advertise in the newspapers that they're going after somebody. They want to keep it as quiet as legally possible, because they know their depositors would not feel safe depositing their money in a bank that just lost a ton in bad loans.

That's why loan officers ask as many questions as they can in order to get a good feel for their potential clients. Remember, they are using their depositors' money and they have to be as careful as possible. They need to use financial information along with the character of the person to make sure that the money they're renting out will be repaid with interest.

A bank loan officer is going to be careful because of the bank's exposure to risk, is much higher than, say, a car dealers. When the car dealer sells you the car and has the money, and possibly your trade-in, his deal is finished. He has given you his product and you've given him your money. (If you haven't given him money, then you get a loan from the bank and he still get his money, so that his deal is usually complete. In some cases, the dealer will be required to co-sign your loan and if you go bad, he is forced to pay. This is called "full recourse paper.") That money, whether cash or loan or some combination, includes the dealer's profit, and everyone's happy.

The difference with banks, as compared to a retailer, is that they are giving you their product, and they have to wait for the return of that product – and their profit. When you bought the car, the dealer got his profit right then.

But loans don't work like that. You have the bank's product, the loan, and if you take its product and skip town, it has to chase you down to retrieve the product and the profit. That can be difficult and expensive, so the loan officer will want to make sure that you are the kind of person who will not run off with the bank's money and will pay the interest on it.

So, remember, when you're applying for credit, always put your best foot forward. If it's just an application, try to type the application or print it very legibly and neatly with a ballpoint pen – don't put arrows around the sides or use a pen that skips or blots. Make it neat. If you're going in for a personal interview, be composed. Look neat and clean and you'll make a good impression. This will go a long, long way in helping you obtain your loan.

Submitting, Tracking and Recording the Results of Your Applications

By now, your application should be filled in completely. Wherever spaces are blank because the information is not available or the question is not applicable, put in "N/A." N/A means Not Applicable or Not Available, and shows the loan officer that you read that question and weren't avoiding it and hadn't overlooked it. He understands that the information is not available or applicable to that particular circumstance. This way, you likely won't get back a decline letter stating that you have sent in an incomplete application. So, when you're ready to apply, just review your application and make sure everything is filled out and that it's neat. Also, make sure that it agrees with the information on your master application.

You then need to set up a tracking chart. You can either copy the one we've supplied at the end of this Chapter or make one that's convenient for you. Just keep track of when you send out your applications, what credit bureaus check your credit, whether you've been approved or declined, and whether you're going to recontact those banks.

In most cases, you should recontact the banks if the reason for the rejection is minor, such as excessive inquiries. With excessive inquiries, you can write to the bank, saying that you're active in the business community and any normal, active businessperson has a lot of inquiries on his account. As long as your credit report is in good shape, the bank may overlook the inquiries.

Again, this is a hit or miss thing. Sometimes you win, sometimes you don't, but if you don't try you'll never know. All we're trying to do in this book is to stack the odds in your favor.

We're simply putting the odds in your favor by telling you the specific ways to contact and recontact banks and showing you the inner workings of these organizations. Even though you're dealing with institutions and organizations, there are real people actually computing your records and making the final decisions as to whether or not to grant you credit. By recontacting a bank and writing a simple letter or calling on the phone, you can do wonders and people will think more of your character because you made that little extra effort. So, keep track of what happens and make sure you recontact the banks to learn the specific reasons why you've been declined, so that you can try and overcome those declines. To your amazement, you may find that many of those institutions that have declined your application will change their minds.

Forgotten or Overlooked Small Loan Sources

People who need money often overlook assets that have cash value.

For example:

Insurance policies: Some have a value that you can tap.

Paid-for vehicles: Often you can borrow several thousand dollars, using the vehicle as collateral.

Jewelry: Often a diamond or other expensive jewelry can be used as collateral.

Use your own imagination. Maybe there are some things around the house that you don't use anymore that you could sell. Perhaps you have a barbecue grill that might be worth a couple hundred dollars or a VCR. If you can get $400, $500, $600 or $1,000 for these items, then you won't need to borrow.

This is often all you have to do to get back on your feet. Moreover, you'll feel a lot better about it by doing it yourself.

Use your thinking cap and try to figure out what items you could liquidate or mortgage to raise a few dollars. It doesn't have to be a substantial amount – sometimes as little as $500 will do the trick, and the way prices are today, it shouldn't be too difficult to raise. If you find yourself in that situation, get out there and go to it.

Credit for Women and Minorities

In 1975, the Equal Credit Opportunity Act was passed, making it illegal to discriminate on the basis of sex or marital status. The law protects women regarding the following issues:

1. A creditor has to consider any alimony, child support, or separate mainte-nance as legitimate income as long as the payments are reliable. Creditors have their own ideas as to what constitutes reliability, so you have to ask what evidence or proof they want before you apply. You don't have to reveal any income that comes from these sources unless you think you won't obtain your credit unless you do.

2. A creditor may not require you to reapply for credit because you are divorced, widowed, separated, or married, or because you changed your name. However, a creditor may require that you change the terms of your account.

3. A creditor cannot refuse to consider any income that comes from regu-lar part-time work.

4. A creditor may not ask what your marital status is if you're applying for a separate unsecured account unless you live in a community property state such as Louisiana, New Mexico, Texas, or Washington. If you don't live in one of those states, and you're not relying on your spouse's income or child support, and your spouse will not be using the account, the credit grantor cannot ask for any information about your spouse. Creditors cannot require your husband to co-sign or guarantee credit on a loan unless you are depending on his income to support your application or unless jointly held property is used as collateral for a secured loan. When you're applying for credit, you do not have to use Miss, Mrs., or Ms. with your name. Creditors cannot ask any questions about birth control practices, or your desire to have children. They cannot assume that your income will drop if you have children.

Filing a Discrimination Complaint

If you feel a lending institution has violated your rights under the Equal Credit Opportunity Act, you should immediately file a formal complaint with the appropriate governmental agency.

If your complaint is against a state-chartered bank:

Director, Division of Consumer and Community Affairs
Board of Governors of the Federal Reserve System
Washington, D.C. 20551

If your complaint is against a national bank:

      Comptroller of the Currency

      Consumer Affairs Division

      Washington, D.C. 20219

If your complaint is against a non-member insured bank:

      Federal Deposit Insurance Corporation

      Office of Bank Customer Affairs

      Washington, D.C. 20429

A Financial Planning Outline

Whenever you apply for credit, you should first have an accurate picture of your financial situation. It is of paramount importance to know exactly where and how your money is being spent. Be sure to complete the Personal Budget Worksheet in the sample section at the end of this chapter.

## CREDIT SCORING GUIDELINES CHART

| FACTORS | POINTS | YOUR SCORE |
|---|---|---|
| MARITAL STATUS | | |
| Married | 1 | _____ |
| Not married | 0 | _____ |
| AGE | | |
| 21 to 25 | 0 | _____ |
| 26 to 64 | 1 | _____ |
| 65 & over | 0 | _____ |
| MONTHLY INCOME: | | |
| Up to $600 | 1 | _____ |
| $601 to $800 | 2 | _____ |
| $601 to $1,000 | 4 | _____ |
| over $1,001 | 6 | _____ |
| YEARS ON THE JOB: | | |
| Less than one | 0 | _____ |
| 1 to 3 | 1 | _____ |
| 4 to 6 | 2 | _____ |
| over 7 | 3 | _____ |
| OCCUPATION: | | |
| Unskilled | 1 | _____ |
| Skilled | 2 | _____ |
| Professional | 3 | _____ |
| IN ADDITION: | | |
| Phone in your name | 2 | _____ |
| Checking or Savings | 2 | _____ |
| MONTHLY OBLIGATIONS: | | |
| 0 to $200 | 1 | _____ |
| Over $200 | 0 | _____ |
| CREDIT HISTORY: | | |
| Loan at this bank | 4 | _____ |
| Other bank loans | 2 | _____ |
| RESIDENCE: | | |
| Rent unfurnished | 1 | _____ |
| Without mortgage | 4 | _____ |
| Own with mortgage | 3 | _____ |
| Any other | 0 | _____ |
| DEPENDENTS: | | |
| 1 to 3 | 1 | _____ |
| Over 3 | 0 | _____ |
| No Dependents | 0 | _____ |
| PREVIOUS RESIDENCE: | | |
| 0 to 5 Years | 0 | _____ |
| 6 Years or over | 1 | _____ |

## POINT SCORING SYSTEM

| CATEGORY | POINTS |
|---|---|

**Age Group:**

18-25 . . . . . . . . . . . . . . . . . . . . . . . . . . . . . . . . 1

26-64 . . . . . . . . . . . . . . . . . . . . . . . . . . . . . . . . 2

65 &up ............................................... 1

**DEPENDENTS:**

None............................................... 0

1-3 . . . . . . . . . . . . . . . . . . . . . . . . . . . . . . . . 2

4 or more ........................................... 1

**STABILITY:**

Up to 5 years at present address...........................1

Over 5 years at present address...........................2

**Years at Previous Address:**

Less than 5 years..................................... 1

More than 5 years .................................... 2

**EMPLOYMENT:**

Less than 1 year at present employment.................... 1

1-3 years at present employment............................. 2

4-6 years at present employment............................. 3

7-10 years at present employment............................ 4

Over 10 years at present employment........................ 5

Spouse employed, if applying jointly........................... 2

Telephone listed in applicant's name ....................... 2

**LOAN EXPERIENCE:**

At bank where you are applying for loan.................... 5

At another bank.......................................3

Checking or savings account at same bank .............. 3

At another bank.......................................2

**TYPE OF EMPLOYMENT:**

Professional/Executive....................................4

Skilled Worker ........................................3

Blue Collar ..........................................2

All Others............................................ 1

**MONTHLY OBLIGATIONS (including rent/mortgage):**

Less than $250........................................ 2

More than $250 ...................................... 1

## Sample Letter of Recommendation

# John Q. Lawyer

Attorney At Law

Any Town, USA  00000

GENERAL PRACTICE
FAMILY LAW
TRIAL PRACTICE-GENERAL

To Whom It May Concern:

I have known Mary Smith and been a customer of her business, Hats By Mary,
for quite some time. I have always found Ms. Smith to be honest, forthright and industrious. She has made numerous improvements in the business and expanded her merchandise. I feel the prospects for her and her business are bright.

John Q. Lawyer

Sample Letter Of Recommendation

ANY REALTORS            MAIN OFFICE
ASSOCIATES, INC.        ANY TOWN


To Whom It May Concern:

I have been a satisfied customer of Mary Smith's Hat Shop since her purchase of the business.

During that time, I have seen the quality, variety, and quantity of the inventory increase dramatically. Mary's personality has also contributed to the growth of her business, in that she is courteous, dependable, and accommodating to her customers.

She has brought the business a long way, and I'm sure she will continue to prosper because of her excellent service and competitive prices.

Sincerely,


John P. Realtor

Sample Letter Of Recommendation

# ANY TOWN CHAMBER OF COMMERCE, INC

To Whom it May Concern:

I have known Mary Smith, owner of Hats By Mary, for the past two years.

I am a frequent visitor and customer of this store not only for the past two years, but for the past nine years. I have seen this store flounder, have mis management and no aggressiveness in the previous seven years before Mary took over the store.

Since Mary took the store over, about two years ago, she has re-vamped, re-arranged, promoted, added new items for sale and worked hard in order to make this store a profitable operation. Mary has a very optimistic and tremendous personality that I believe helps her a great deal with her relationships with customers.

I personally feel that Hats by Mary, under Mary's management, is a real asset to our business community.

Sincerely,


Any Town County
Chambers of Commerce, Inc.

## SAMPLE TRACKING RECORD

| Name of Bank or Savings & Loan | Date of Applications | Credit Bureau | Approved | Declined | Recontact |
|---|---|---|---|---|---|
|  |  |  |  |  |  |
|  |  |  |  |  |  |
|  |  |  |  |  |  |
|  |  |  |  |  |  |
|  |  |  |  |  |  |
|  |  |  |  |  |  |
|  |  |  |  |  |  |
|  |  |  |  |  |  |
|  |  |  |  |  |  |
|  |  |  |  |  |  |
|  |  |  |  |  |  |
|  |  |  |  |  |  |
|  |  |  |  |  |  |
|  |  |  |  |  |  |
|  |  |  |  |  |  |
|  |  |  |  |  |  |
|  |  |  |  |  |  |
|  |  |  |  |  |  |
|  |  |  |  |  |  |
|  |  |  |  |  |  |
|  |  |  |  |  |  |
|  |  |  |  |  |  |
|  |  |  |  |  |  |
|  |  |  |  |  |  |
|  |  |  |  |  |  |
|  |  |  |  |  |  |
|  |  |  |  |  |  |
|  |  |  |  |  |  |
|  |  |  |  |  |  |
|  |  |  |  |  |  |
|  |  |  |  |  |  |
|  |  |  |  |  |  |

# Personal Budget Worksheet

|  | Projected | Actual | Difference |
|---|---|---|---|
| **Income** |  |  |  |
| Salaries | $ | $ | $ |
| Wages from self-employment |  |  |  |
| Dividends & Interest |  |  |  |
| Rental |  |  |  |
| Alimony |  |  |  |
| Other |  |  |  |
| **Total Income** | $ | $ | $ |
| **Fixed Expenses** |  |  |  |
| Food | $ | $ | $ |
| Housing |  |  |  |
| Utilities |  |  |  |
| Transportation |  |  |  |
| Maintenance |  |  |  |
| Clothing & furnishings |  |  |  |
| Installment purchases |  |  |  |
| Insurance premiums |  |  |  |
| Medical & dental care |  |  |  |
| Education |  |  |  |
| Taxes (property, federal, state, and local) |  |  |  |
| Personal care and other |  |  |  |
| **Total Fixed Expenses** | $ | $ | $ |
| **Total Available After Fixed Expenses** | $ | $ | $ |
| **Variable Expenses** |  |  |  |
| Entertainment & recreation | $ | $ | $ |
| Vacations |  |  |  |
| Savings |  |  |  |
| Investments |  |  |  |
| Other |  |  |  |
| **Total Variable Expenses** | $ | $ | $ |
| **Total Available at End of Month** | $ | $ | $ |

# CHAPTER 4

## CREDIT BUREAUS

The Three Major Credit Bureaus

In this chapter, we're going to discuss credit bureaus. We'll begin with a look at the 3 major credit bureaus. As of this printing, Experian, CBI/Equifax and TransUnion operate nationwide. The following are the addresses and telephone numbers of these three major credit bureaus. Please verify the correct address by calling the credit bureau prior to sending checks or information in the mail due to the fact that the credit bureaus frequently change their "dispute" addresses.

EXPERIAN                    Website – www.experian.com

Experian

P.O. Box 2104

Allen, TX. 75013-2104

1-888-EXPERIAN

1-888-397-3742

When sending for a copy of your credit report remember that you may qualify for a free report if you have been turned down for credit within the past 60 days.

If you were turned down for credit, make a copy of your denial letter and send it to the credit bureau where your credit was originally pulled. They will send you a current copy of your report within 30 days.

Should you be paying for a copy of your credit report via mail you will need to send in the following information for security purposes:

## 1. FULL NAME:

INCLUDING MIDDLE INITIAL AND GENERATION
Example:   Salvatore (NOT SAL) J. Manilla (JR/SR/ETC.)

## 2. SPOUSES NAME:

Not always needed – I recommend NOT sending it in unless you are requesting a joint report.

## 3. PRESENT ADDRESS:

Send in your FULL current address including apt. #, suite # or any other characteristics that you would normally use in your address. Let them know how long you have resided there.

## 4. PREVIOUS ADDRESSES:

List your previous addresses for the last 5 years and put a date for each residence.

## 5. TWO (2) PROOFS OF ADDRESS:

Phone bill, electric bill, driver's license (I don't recommend using your driver's license).

## 6. DATE OF BIRTH (DOB)

This is very important because there are many people with the same name but they usually have different birthdays and different ss#'s.

## 7. SOCIAL SECURITY #:

Make certain to double-check your ss# prior to sending this info to the bureau because if you made a mistake it might show up as "FRAUD ALERT" On your credit report. Why? Because now the credit bureau has two different ss#'s on file.

Type all this information out neatly and send it, along with your check, to the address listed above. You should have your report within 45 days.

You can also order your report over the internet. Go to their website and follow the instructions.

<u>Trans Union</u>        Website – www.transunion.com

Trans Union, LLC

Consumer Disclosure Center

P.O. Box 1000

Chester, PA. 19022

Trans Unions asks for slightly different information then Experian. Here is the list of information that Trans Union requests for verification.

FIRST, MIDDLE AND LAST NAME (INCLUDING JR., SR. 111)

CURRENT ADDRESS

PREVIOUS ADDRESS IN PAST 2 YEARS, IF ANY

SOCIAL SECURITY NUMBER

DATE OF BIRT H

CURRENT EMPLOYER

PHONE NUMBER (I NEVER INCLUDE THIS)

SIGNITURE

APPLICABLE FEE

<u>CBI/Equifax</u>

Equifax

P.O. Box 105873

Atlanta, GA. 30348

Website: www.eqifax.com

1-800-685-1111 to order credit report by mail

1-888-766-0008 to report fraud on your credit report

1-800-567-8688 to opt-out for direct mail from Equifax

Equifax did not mention what information they wanted in order to send out your report, but you can assume that it is similar to the information listed above for the other bureaus.

Don't forget to enclose the correct fee. We have not listed the fees here, because they change regularly. Contact each credit bureau for the appropriate fees.

Remember, your credit report is your sole responsibility! Besides creditors, you are the only person who may have your credit report changed, dispute the information on it, or add to it. It is your responsibility to review your credit report and have it updated, corrected, or changed. Generally, a credit file is generated on you the first time you apply for credit. It is the creditor's request for information that creates the file. Not all creditors report to these major reporting agencies. Many report to small local credit bureaus because they charge much lower subscription rates than those charged by the big credit agencies. However, a non-subscribing creditor may elect to purchase a report to gain information on an applicant seeking a large real estate loan or a large lease.

It is surprising how many people do not know that every time they apply for major credit, their credit report is reviewed to determine credit history, credit-worthiness, and character. Most people are unaware of both the kind and quantity of personal information that is contained in their files, or of the individuals and organizations that are reviewing them.

What Is a Credit Bureau?

Most creditors want to know your credit history before they extend new or major credit to you. To obtain this information, they use three major sources: Experian, TransUnion, and CBI.

These are the three major credit reporting agencies in the United States. There are hundreds of smaller local credit bureaus as well. A credit bureau is a clearinghouse that collects and stores information about your credit history.

Not all the information, or all the credit you have, will necessarily be on file with these reporting agencies. The credit grantors provide the bureaus with "factual" information on how their customers pay their bills, and the bureaus then assemble information from each credit report into a credit file.

If you have filed for bankruptcy protection under Chapter 7, 11, or 13, it will be reflected on your report. If you are delinquent in paying your bills, that will show, too. Your report will also reflect good credit. In addition to your financial history, your file may contain other information that creditors may consider important. For example, if you have committed a felony, it may appear on your credit report.

Credit bureaus do not, however, evaluate your creditworthiness. Based upon the factual information accumulated by a credit reporting agency, the credit grantors – not the bureaus themselves – decide whether to grant you credit. Credit grantors extend credit based on their own standards and policies. These may vary greatly from one creditor to another and are also relative to market conditions.

Free Credit Reports

Even if you are unable to turn a declined application around, the added information you receive by recontacting creditors will help you play the credit game better. You will learn what adjustments to make on future applications. Use the decline to get additional information from the credit bureau. You are entitled to know why you were declined, so you must be given a free copy of your credit report upon request. Any credit bureau that services a creditor that declines you is required by law to make you aware of the information on your credit report at no charge to you. When you receive your letter of decline, if it involves a credit report, the creditor must give you the name and address of the credit bureau that issued the report. Simply make a photocopy of your letter of decline and mail it to the credit bureau along with a request for your credit file. Sign your name and provide your Social Security number on your letter of request.

The Fair Credit Report Act gives you the right to know information that has been placed on your credit report. Credit bureaus generally charge anywhere from $2 to $25, but when you are refused credit you are entitled to the information at no cost. The law does not require a credit bureau to provide you with a copy of your credit report – only to make you aware of what is on it. However, most large credit bureaus do their communication with consumers via printed matter rather than telephone.

It is worthwhile to contact the credit bureau that sent the report because you may be able to get the bureau to send a copy of the corrected, more favorable report. For example, an applicant received a decline for "insufficient credit file." This particular bureau didn't cover the area where he lived, and therefore their credit file on him was insufficient. He asked the bureau to contact his local credit bureau, and it was able to update its file and give the bank a favorable credit report.

Understanding and Evaluating Your Credit Report (refer to Credit Report on pages 71-74)

We have included a copy of a credit report from CBI of Sarasota at the end of this chapter. We are using the CBI report because it is one of the easier reports from which to learn and evaluate information. There will also be a copy of a TransUnion report.

We have numbered the important items on the credit report. Most of the other items are self-explanatory. For example, look in the upper left corner of the actual report (the page that says "Confidential" on the upper right corner). It gives you the name of the credit bureau, the address, and an ABC of A. That has nothing to do with us. It is coded information for the credit reporting bureau. Then you have your request date and the date that it was mailed to you. Everything else in this section of the report is self-explanatory.

There are several pages that are dedicated to a step-by-step walk-through of the CBI reports. But first, please take a quick look at the copies of the reports at the end of this chapter.

Let's walk through the CBI report carefully, discussing each item in detail. This will give you a good understanding of the "game." Be sure to refer back to the corresponding numbered item in the report itself. Here we go:

Page 1 of Report

1.      Consumer Code. It says "for" then it has a code, and then it has "Revised Copy August 6." That code is your consumer code. That code shows that it is a consumer copy or a consumer service, whatever the last transaction was. If it was for a bank, they would have that bank code there. When you get your code, it's going to have either a consumer copy code or a consumer service code. That code will match what's on the last page where it says inquiries. When you get your report, those numbers should match.

2       Former Address. It has former address and then it says CRT reported 10/87. What that means is that it's a corrected report. In 10/87 the person corrected the address. Often, if you leave out a simple little thing in your address, such as an East, or South, or your ZIP code, it's going to show up as two or three former addresses. It looks strange when you have a lot of former addresses and they're all the same one. So, for the sake of neatness, it is easier to make one main application and copy the information from it. This way you won't skip a letter or a number.

3.      Firm Identification Code. You'll see an explanation of trade line or explanation of everything that is on your report on the following pages. Everything will be explained in simple layman's English. The Firm Identification Code is the reporting business. A name and a number are normally used. Go down that column and you'll see who is reporting you on a regular basis. For example, in this particular report, the first line is "Chemical." They have the code number they use, and you can see that there are two Chemical accounts on top of each other. They both have the same code. If you look all the way down at the bottom of that first page, you'll see there's another Chemical account that also has the same code. With that particular bank there were three accounts. They report the same code for all the accounts. That is their code. This way they can easily be identified. Sometimes the name does not get punched in every month when it is reported. It might be just a clerical error when the typist forgets to report that information. The only thing that will show up is the code name. There are code books to identify who that is.

4.  Date Reported. It gives the month and year that the information was reported to CBI. All the information shown about this account is as of this date. That is the last date that the account has been reported to CBI. You will see the two Chemical Banks were both reported as of November 1987. On the next line you will see the Freedom Account was last report- ed in September 1987. Sometimes these institutions will report every month whether or not you have any activity on your account. Usually these institutions will consider activity as making a purchase or taking a cash advance, but they will not consider making a payment as an activity. If you go all the way to the right under account number, you will see letters that say DLA. That stands for Date of Last Activity and that matches the 9/87 for the Freedom. If you go across on the Chemical listing and you look at the DLA, you will see that the Date of Last Activity on those are 8/87, but they have reported every month since. Each institution has its own way of reporting and you can see the date that it has reported you last just by looking down the account number column.

5.  Date Opened. This never changes. It's the month and the year in which your account was opened with that lender.

6.  "H.C." This is the Highest amount Charged or the credit limit that you have. Some institutions will report what your credit limit is, and some will report the most you have ever charged on that account. Notice on this report that Chemical Bank is not reporting what the high credit is. Normally they'll say, "amount in HC column is the credit limit." For example, go down to #16 on the left side of the report. It says, "amount in HC column is credit limit." What that's telling you is that's the limit and the account is approximately $240 under the limit on that card. (Just take the high credit limit and subtract the actual balance of $3,004 in column 8, and you will see that the account is about $240 under the limit.) Where it says Chemical Bank in the first column, #14 going across, the HC could either stand for the most ever charged or the credit limit. The only way

that the credit grantor reviewing your application would know if the HC was your credit limit or if it was the highest amount charged is if it specifically says amount in HC column is the credit limit. Otherwise they don't know whether that limit could be $5,000 or $10,000 or whatever amount. Sometimes Chemical Bank reports it as the credit limit and sometimes it doesn't. These are gray areas. In every business, people sometimes make mistakes, and they forget or overlook doing things because they get tired. You sit at a computer terminal for eight hours a day and you start getting a little buggy. You do that day in and day out and you begin to make errors. These people are very fast and usually very accurate, but there is always room for some type of an error. Sometimes it's a minor error, but it can affect you in a major way. Since credit is so important in today's society, it is very important that this financial tool is used properly. If you were a plumber, you wouldn't think of going into somebody's house to work on the piping with a sledgehammer. You would take wrenches and screw- drivers and approved tools to do the job properly. Similarly, in order to do the job properly in the credit and business world, you need to have the prop- er tools. The only way you can have the proper tools is by taking responsibility and making sure that everything is accurate on your credit report.

7.    "TRM." That stands for Terms. These are the terms of the account which you agreed upon and can be represented as either an amount due per month, or a number of months. Once again, this is something that you have to become accustomed to. It's quite simple though, because usually the companies that are reporting months will place a little "m" after the number. That will show that it is usually an installment loan. For example, where it says Chemical #14, under TRM, it says $128. As of the last time that information was reported, it shows what the minimum payment due was. That doesn't mean that is what was paid. It could have been $300 or $500 or could have paid off the entire balance. For that billing cycle that was the amount of the minimum monthly payment. The next line down is $21 and that shows what the payment was on that account.

That payment could go up if more was charged. However, if the subject paid that loan down to half the amount, it is possible that the next monthly payment would be approximately half and that would show up as $10 the following month. If you go down the TRM column, you'll see online number 19 Avco Financial. You'll see that it says "36m." That doesn't stand for $36,000. It stands for 36 months. That means that is an installment loan. Where an installment loan differs from a revolving account is that on those Chemical accounts or any of those others where there is no term, the subject can borrow more money if they like and they'll just add that to the monthly payment. They can borrow up to their credit limit. However, on the Avco Financial, that tells you exactly what the high cred- it was, which was a fixed amount. This can't change unless the subject goes back to Avco and reapplies for more money, which is not as flexible as a revolving account. What they do is fix your payments and it doesn't say how much my payments are here. All it says is that it's for 36 months. So, if somebody wanted to figure out what your payments were, they would need to take the amount of your high credit, which was $2,193 in this instance, and divide it by 36 months. They'll come up with a fairly accurate amount of what's due every month.

8.    BAL. That stands for the balance. That shows the amount that's owed on the account at the time that it was reported to CBI. That doesn't necessarily mean that's what your balance is at the moment. You may have paid off the entire balance on your last billing cycle, and it didn't get entered in the computer soon enough, so you'll be showing a balance of several thousand dollars when actually your balance is zero. If you are applying for a loan and you want to show that some of these accounts are paid down to zero, yet you know that they are not going to show up that way on your report, you can do one of two things: either wait an additional month until the account actually shows zero; or pay these accounts with money orders and make photo copies of the money orders showing the payments. Then send that into the credit bureau and they'll automatically put in a zero bal-

ance if you can prove that the payment has been made. The best thing to do is to keep investigating. Always look for more information on credit, credit reporting procedures, and anything that comes your way in newspapers or magazines, or on television. Never stop learning. Always look for another way, because even as this information is being reported, changes are taking place. Keep on top of it. As far as the balance goes, that just shows how much balance you have as of that date. If you go down the BAL column, you'll see a zero. Go over to the left, you'll see that's #18 - Barnett Bank. Barnett Bank was originally a $30,000 loan. It says 30k. The "k" stands for thousands. In this instance they forgot to put in the term, which was $812 per month. A subsequent loan or a rollover that was in the original agreement was used, and you'll see on the next line that it was paid down to $20,000. This time they listed the amount and the term. It also shows what the balance was as of the date that it was last reported, which was 10/87. If you go down the BAL column and you see a lot of zeros, either it means that the account has been paid down to zero and it's still an active account, or it could mean that the accounts are paid in full. Go down the BAL column on the second page of the report and you will notice that there are a lot of zeros in that balance column. It is good to have a lot of zeros on closed accounts because it shows you paid as agreed, you had a good account, you had lots of accounts, and you've been a good credit customer over the years. Those accounts will stay on your report usually for seven years and sometimes more if you request that they stay on.

9.    PD (Past Due). That is the amount an account is past due as of the date of the last reporting. Most companies don't bother entering an amount unless you are more than 30 days past due. There have been times when you may go away for several weeks. Try to get all your bills paid before you leave. Inevitably there is always a bill that comes in and needs to be paid while you are away. Being only several days late is not a problem as long as your payment is received before the billing date of your next state-

ment. There is also a little friendly reminder because they realize that payments often are in the mail. If you are late, call customer service and ask them if they've entered your payment. Ask, "Is this going to reflect negatively on my credit report?" Usually they say, "No, you have a very good account," and "Yes, we received your payment a couple of days after the due date." If the minimum monthly payment the month before was $50 and the next month the minimum monthly payment $50 plus the $50 that was overdue, they would put the minimum monthly payment of $100 as the total minimum payment. Well, since they already received a payment of $50 from the month before, it is not necessary that the entire $100 be forwarded. Confirm that with them on the phone. All you have to do is send in the current month's minimum payment of $50. However, don't pay your bills past the due date because not every creditor is exactly the same. Some banks won't include the interest they charge as part of your credit line, but most do.

10. CS. Look on the first page of the report. "CS" stands for Current Status and the type of account that you have. The only way that you can decode that information is to read the explanation of trade line on the attached sheet that comes with every report. On the right side where it says, "Terms of Sale" and "Current Manner of Payment," it will tell you in those squares exactly what it stands for. If you look down at the accounts, you'll see all "R 1" s and "I 1" s. "R 1" stands for revolving or option, open-ended account. A revolving account is usually just a credit card or an account on which you can borrow up to your credit line any time you want. The balance is solely up to your discretion up to the credit limit. It is not an installment loan on which the amount is fixed, and you have to make fixed monthly payments. Go down to #18, which is Barnett Bank. It says "I 1" in the CS column. That stands for Installment. This tells you that those are fixed monthly payments. If people want to find out whether that's just the amount you're paying for that month as a minimum monthly payment, or it's a fixed amount, all they need to do is look at your current status and

figure out whether you're paying in installments or on a revolving account. If it's an installment, it means that the monthly installments are the same every month. It's easy enough to see how long it's going to take for that account to be paid off. If it's revolving, they have no way of knowing if that account will ever be paid down to zero, and it's just another way of determining when your debts will be cleared, if any. The "l" stands for the current manner of payment. It goes from 0 to 9. "O" stands for "too new to rate" which means it is a brand-new account and you haven't established a rating, or it stands for approved but not used. It goes with any account whether it's an open-ended, revolving, or installment account. You'll find that R, 0, or I before that number, and that tells you what type of account it is. The number tells you what your payment history was. You will notice that all of the accounts are a "l" at this point, which means that payments have been made within 30 days of billing and the accounts have been paid as agreed. Look on the second page and you'll notice there's an "R O" for Eastern Airlines. It's not because it's a new account. Look at the date reported, or the date opened, and you'll notice that the account was opened a couple of years ago. The last time they reported was at the time the account was opened. They haven't reported since. They don't report on a regular basis unless the account is being used, and what they're telling the rest of the credit world is that there has been no activity. It's easy enough to figure out just by looking at the date that the account was opened. If the account was opened the same month in which it was reported, and it's only a month or two since the card was issued, then it would look as though the account is just too new to report, but in this instance it's showing that the account has not been used as of time the report was made. If you go back to the first page of the report and look toward the bottom, you'll see an account called Robinson's. If you look across, you'll see that the date it was opened was February '85 and the last date that it was reported was August '87. That account has been open for 2 years. The HC column shows a zero amount. This indicates that there has been no activity. There is no term, and the balance is zero. However they are showing the current status as being "Rl". Even though unused it should be a "RO," some companies will report you as doing things as agreed if you don't do anything at all. That is a gray area again. Every credit grantor and every credit bureau is a little different. When you learn to deal with financial institutions and credit bureaus in a reasonable and educated manner, you will be able to do the things that you need to do. If you let these things slide, they're just going to hurt you more. You need to take care of these things. They're simple, believe it or not. There are a lot of things out there in life that are simple, but not easy. This is simple and it's not that hard. It becomes very easy when you know what you're doing, and you learn how to handle the credit reporting agencies and the banks.

11.    Months Reported. In this column, the first two accounts are Chemical Bank. There is no amount of months being reported. For some reason, they have been left out. We think the reason that they were left out is that the last time the account was checked, they inadvertently reported the months as 6 months instead of 60 months.  If you look at when the account was opened and compare it to the date that it has been reported, it should have been somewhere around 60 months.  The computer operator who was keying in the information made a typographical error on those accounts and put in 06 for six months instead of 60 for 60 months. The agency was asked to change that to 60 months so that it would reflect a more accurate picture of the amount of time. Not that it was major, because anybody who would look over at the date opened and date reported would be able to see that. However, it should be done because the people who are reviewing you for credit are often busy, or it may be just before their lunch break, or before they are ready to go home, and they don't review everything on your application in as detailed a manner as they otherwise would. They may just look for certain things to see how long accounts are open. If they looked in the months reported column, they would see that inaccurate information. Sometimes the credit reporting agency will change these things for you and sometimes it needs to contact the creditors to find out

what is accurate. In this particular situation, the agency just removed it from the report for this particular month. Even on your closed accounts, it will show how many months that account was reported. What is good about that is that if you have an account which appears to be a 36-month account from the date that it was opened, and it shows that you have been reported for 30 months and your balance is paid down to zero, the credit grantor looks at it and will be able to determine that not only did you pay as agreed, but you paid ahead of time. Your account was paid in full before the actual due date on your loan.

12    ECOA. Stands for "Equal Credit Opportunity Act account." That defines the type of participation on the account. You should look at the ECOA code on the explanation of trade line that CBI furnishes with their copies. The Equal Credit Opportunity Act designators explain who is responsible for the account and the type of participation you have with the account. The "J" stands for Joint, the "I" for Individual, "U" for Undesignated, "A" is for Authorized user, "T" is Terminated, "M" is the Maker, "C" is Co- maker, "B" on Behalf of another person, and "S" is Shared. You will notice that most of the accounts are "I" except for the J.C. Penney account on the first page. J.C. Penney is a shared account. That's an account that husband and wife had together, and each had their own cards. Both were responsible for that account. In the event that either had died, or run away, or not wanted to pay the bills anymore, the other would have been responsible for the remaining balance. This is called Jointly and Severally. You want to try to get most of your ECOA accounts as Individual because that shows that you are the sole person responsible for that account. If the accounts are in good shape, then it shows up as a very positive rating on your behalf. If most of your accounts are Shared, Undesignated, or Joint, it makes it more difficult for the credit grantor to determine whether you have actually been making those payments yourself. Sometimes some- body else who is responsible for the account doesn't want to see it go into a bad rating and makes the payments. So, try to get everything  designated

as Individual. Another reason to keep everything individual, especially in today's society, is that during a divorce, people will often become quite agitated and nasty. For example, if spouses decide to get back at their husbands or wives, they can take a shared or joint credit card and charge it up to the limit, or take a cash advance out and then not pay the bills. The best thing to do is to get your own individual accounts not only because of the reasons given, but in the event that one partner dies It makes it a lot easier if you each have your own individual credit and can stand on your own two feet. If it ever comes to a divorce, or a spouse dies, then the remaining spouse has his or her own credit. This is not to say that you shouldn't share some accounts, but on those accounts that you share, try not to make them your major credit cards.  If one of you gets hurt and the income stops coming in, all of your accounts will get hurt if you can't afford to pay them. At least, if one of you gets hurt and you have individual accounts, you can target one person's accounts to become delinquent and work on those at a later date.  It makes it a lot easier and a lot simpler if you have a plan ahead of time. People, in general, don't plan to fail, we just fail to plan.

13. Account Number. If you go down the account number column, you will notice that some of the account numbers have been blackened out because those are real credit cards and account numbers.  The numbers show which account number you are being reported on. For example, on the report on the first page, you will see the two Chemical Banks. The top Chemical Bank, where it says 4114, tells you that it is a Visa card. Then it has the branch number, which is 206. The rest is the account number for that Visa card. On the second Chemical Bank, the 5263 shows that it is a MasterCard, and that the branch's number is 206. The rest of the numbers that are blackened out constitute the account number. Look at #15. That is the date of the last activity on those particular accounts. Every one of the accounts on the CBI report has a date of last activity.  Two lines are permitted for each account. Not everybody takes up the two lines, but usually they will. If you want to check any of your account numbers to

make sure they are accurate with what appears on your billing statements, that is easy enough to do. Pull out your last monthly bill, look up your account number and check to be sure it matches. That is just another way of identifying which account they are reporting on.

14.     That is over on the left side of Page 1. That information will be going across the page instead of up and down. Once again we will just review this. It will tell you the name of the institution reporting on you, the firm identification code, the date that this has been reported, the date that they opened the account, then your high credit, your term, how much you are paying, your present balance, if you have any past due amounts or not, the current status (in this case it is Rl), what the months reported are (there is nothing reported there), your ECOA (code which in this case is individual), then the account number. On the next line you will see that it is blank all the way over to the date of last activity, which is normally what would be in that second line. Under firm identification code would be a series of numbers of 30, 60, or 90, which would show how many times the per- son has been 30 days past due, 60 days past due, or 90 days past due.

15.     Date of Last Activity. On this particular account the date of last activity was 8/87 even though the date that they last reported was 11/87.

16.     Amount in HC Column is Credit Limit. That usually goes on top of your account. Sometimes they will take up as many as three lines. For example, this one says amount in HC column is the credit limit. That goes for the First Select account and it shows 3241. We don't believe there was that much credit on that account, but that is what they came up with and it's OK, because that is pretty close to what the credit limit is anyway. Then you will see that on the next line it has the date of last activity. So, in that instance they used three lines. Usually they take two lines.

17.     Once again, this is just the account number for the account opened with

them. It makes it easier to figure out what's going on – especially if you have more than one account with the same institution. There are two on the top and one on the bottom of Page 1. You can determine which is which by looking at the numbers. If you look down on the bottom line, where it says months reported, it says 64. You will notice that account was opened as of December '81 and the other account was opened in January '82. When they issued the Visa card and MasterCard at the same time, they misspelled the applicant's name on the Visa card, and it was returned. They opened that account a month later.

18.    Barnett Bank. You'll notice over in the high credit, it says 30K. That stands for thousands. They don't have enough room to put in 30,000.

19.    Avco Financial. Years ago, people would go to these institutions when they were turned down by a conventional lender. The interest rate on these accounts was usually several percentage points higher than at a conventional bank, because they lend to people who cannot get conventional loans – to people who generally are higher credit risks. When there is a higher credit risk, there is a higher rate of defaulting on loans, and the only way these institutions make money is by charging the higher interest rate to cover the higher losses they incur. In recent years, however, Avco Financial and Beneficial and many of these other secondary sources have come full swing and are now in competition with many of the savings and loans and banking institutions because they offer more attractive terms. However, they still get a little bit more interest. One of the things these lenders tell you is that they charge simple interest. This means that it's not compounded interest – it's just simple interest charged on your outstanding balance. They used to send you a bill every time you made a payment as long as it was before the next payment due. For example, if your payment was due on the first of every month and you sent it in on the 15th of the month, by the 20th of that month you would already have your next bill showing the amount of interest and principal paid. If you immediate-

ly made another payment on that statement, your next payment due date wouldn't be for two months and most of your payment would have been applied towards the principal. Most of your second payment would have gone toward principal and very little toward interest because your payments were so close together. Then if you waited the full two months to make your next payment (say it was a $100 payment), $85 to $90 might go toward interest, and only $10 or $15 would go toward principal. Now they bill customers monthly, regardless of when the payment was made. If you make your payment the day after the bill comes, you're still not going to receive another statement for 30 days.

20.   Here's something that's fairly important. It says the consumer copy of the credit file is not to be used as a credit report. You'll notice that on any copy that you receive. We imagine the main reason they do this is because they don't want you to give your report to different financial institutions and tell them that it's accurate, when it is probably easy enough for someone to take a typewriter or a computer and add or delete information. If a person were able to get some of these confidential sheets printed up himself, he could put whatever information he wanted on them. Financial institutions and lending institutions will not generally take the report that you submit to them as being true and accurate. They may review and make a decision as to whether or not they'll lend you money based on it as long as the report they pull up is the same report. However, they usually will not accept a report from you as the final word.

Page 2 of Report

21.   BK-l- COL-VI * 1480N28. That is a Bank One credit card, and the numbers are the company's identification code. That's just some coding they use and if you'll look over to where it says, "amount in HC column is credit limit," it says $30. Could you imagine a bank issuing a credit card with only a $30 limit? It's obvious that's another mistake. This just proves there are a lot of little errors made by people who are punching in infor-

mation on you every day. The only way that you can keep on top of it is to continuously get credit reports and do your homework.

22.     Here's another Avco loan. All it says is Avco. It doesn't say Avco Financial. The only way you would know whether or not it's the same institution that's on the front is by matching up the numbers. Since those numbers don't match up, it means it's a different Avco Financial reporting. You'll notice that their code numbers are very different. They transferred the account to another branch which was closer to the borrower's home. This is how the subject began doing business with Avco Financial: Avco sent a pre-approved letter and said it would lend up to $2,500 if he came in and signed. At that time, he wanted to establish more credit on his report in the area, so he borrowed approximately $2,000 and paid it back. You'll notice on line #19 of the first page that the account was transferred again. It was transferred back to the original place where he had done business.

23.     This line tells you the account was transferred. From the way it is written on the credit report, it's hard to tell whether it was the Sears account that was transferred or the Avco account.

24.     This is a Sears account. You'll notice it was opened in February 1987, and April 1987 was the date that it was reported. Something that is rather strange is it indicates the high credit is $42, and the balance is $43. The balance is higher than the highest credit limit. Sears reported only one month. A telephone was purchased through one of its catalog stores, and the account was opened so a phone order could be made. When the bill came in it was paid off in full right away. It is still on the report as not being paid off in full. It's only a $43 balance. It shows one month as being reported and it shows that the last date of activity was 10 months ago.

25.     Eastern Airlines.   We've gone over this one briefly.  It shows how much

the credit limit is on that account. The airline feels that's a reasonable amount for the average flier. If the account holder was a frequent flier the airline might give a limit of $2,500 or $5,000 if so requested. It is more or less a limited subscriber rather than an automatic subscriber and it will probably report information only when there's activity on the account.

26. This is a very important line. You'll notice that the information on line 26 doesn't correspond to the way the information in the previous 25 lines has been reported. The reason is that information was added on at a later date and it was not reported directly by those companies to this credit reporting agency. The account holder wrote to the companies and said, "I had a good account with you, it was a credit account, I paid as agreed, so I would appreciate it if you would send the credit bureau at this address the information." The subject wrote out all the information and told them to verify it with their records first and then send it on to the credit reporting agency so that it would show up on the credit report. And that's what they did. He had leased a copy machine for one of his businesses and gave them the date that he opened the account, and the date of last activity. They put down the date that it was opened as 4/84 and the date that it was closed as 12/86. It shows Il – it was an individual account, paid as agreed. The high credit was $1,949. That included all the interest and everything else. The balance now is zero. The date of the last activity was 4/86. That is an account he had added to his credit report. The Manufacturers Hanover Trust was for a motorcycle that he bought when he was younger. It was on the TRW report, but not on the CBI report. He got a copy of his TRW report and circled the account. He sent it into CBI and said, "Here, it's being reported on my TRW, would you please transfer this information onto my CBI report," and that's what they did. CBI put it on the report for him. We skipped over this before, but go back to Page 1, line number 18 and look at that Barnett Bank loan. There are two columns of that Barnett Bank loan. One is for $20,000 and the other is for $30,000. That was a commercial loan for a business. Business loans, commercial loans, and

mortgages are normally not reported to credit reporting agencies at all. The only reason these were included is because the account holder went into the bank after he had paid on the account for several years and asked to have that information put on his report. They sent a "notification serv- ice letter." The type of rating that they gave was an Il. We've included a copy of it at the end of Section 4.4 (this sub-section). They even made a mistake on the dates. You'll notice that it says date of last activity for the second loan of $20,000 was 9/10. That's showing September 1910. In 1910, he hadn't been born. Needless to say, he went to the credit bureau and said, "That's an error." They changed it because they realized that it was a typographical error. It's easy to see now, just by this one report, that there have been at least four or five errors. Nothing major at the time, but errors just the same. Imagine the errors on the report of people who haven't looked at their reports in 10 or 15 years and have no idea of how to read them. They may be denied credit for simple little things over which they had no control. Make sure that you understand the codes and you understand that you need to keep your file up to date. On the notification service sheet that the bank issued, look at the first line, where it reads type and rating Il. Go across to where it says, "terms." It says 11 at 812 and that's telling them that he had 11 payments at $812 a month. The loan was then rolled over and it was 23 payments at $396. This was given to the credit reporting agency, but when they added it to the report, they left out the $812 as the monthly payment on the $30,000 loan. A phone call told them they forgot to put it in, and they corrected it. If you want to keep your report up to date, we suggest that you get your report every three to six months. Don't worry that it shows "consumer copies" and "consumer service" on your report. We doubt that any bank or lending institution would look negatively upon that.

27. Inquiries. Actually, we should have put the 27 balances where it says "No Public Records" for both of them. A public record would be a judgment, or a bankruptcy, or something of that nature. They didn't find anything on

him and they just let them know that is the end of the report. Where it says "Inquiries" it says, "subject shows seven inquiries since 8/87." They usually go back about six months. Most of your inquiries will stay on for two years and then will be dropped. Promotional inquiries will stay on for around six months, but sometimes they don't purge them from the records unless you call and say it needs to be taken off. On the report, in this particular instance, you'll notice that the last three inquiries were 1 consumer copy and 2 consumer services. So, the seven inquiries were actually only four inquiries since 8/87. One of them was a promotion, and one of them was his insurance company.

28. Consumer Service. The Consumer Service has a number next to it. That is a code to show the institution they're dealing with what's going on. That code shows that it is a consumer service. If you'll look on the front of Page 1, up at the top where you see the number 1, those numbers will match. There are a couple of extra zeros up on the front page, but the numbers do match. The reason there was a consumer service done on 11/9 and one done on 10/22, was because when he got his consumer copy on 10/7, he had some minor changes that needed to be made. After they made the changes they sent him a consumer copy. They sent him another copy on 10/22, which was stamped "consumer service" showing that they had made the changes. He found that they hadn't made all of the changes and that some of the things were still not correct. He sent it back to them and they sent him another updated copy on 11/9. That is why there are two consumer services recorded. If he wishes, he could write to them and ask them to please remove one of them. They have done that in the past.

29. Consumer copy. This means that the subject received a copy of his report. A lender should be able to determine if it was because of a denial and a free report was provided, or if it was a paid report. If he looks back over the past 30 to 60 days and sees that someone checked the credit, and then he notices that an account has not been opened, he is going to realize that the

applicant has probably been denied credit, and that he is just sending in for a free copy to see what is going on. If he sees that no one has checked credit in the past couple of months and assumes he got a consumer copy, then he is probably just paying for a copy of the report to stay current.

30.    PRM. That stands for a promotion. Somebody wanted to get the name of people who had good accounts. The actual report is not given to the promotion company at that time because they do not have permission to check your credit at that point. The only way you'll know who offered a promotion is by asking the credit bureau to check that code, and you'll often be surprised at who is looking for your name. It could be a bank in California that is trying to expand its credit card services. They get your name, see what kind of income you have, that you have a good account, and then they may send you a pre-approved credit card. We discussed this a little earlier. They send you a pre-approved card for, say, $3,000, and then all you have to do is fill in your name, your current job, and some- times how much you are earning, sign the bottom and send it back. At that point, they will check your credit, because you signed the bottom of that card, which gives them permission to do so. Within about 30 to 60 days, you will see another inquiry on your report with the name of the banking institution that sent you that pre-approved card. You now have two inquiries within a 60-day period from the same institution. If they are going to issue you a card, they should take that promotion off as soon as the card is issued. If they deny you credit, they ought to take both of them off your credit record because you did not solicit them. Request that they take both inquiries off your credit report. If you don't do that, then you are going to have to live with those two inquiries. It will show that no account is opened and that will affect your report negatively. So, take a little time and a little effort to sit down and write a letter, and ask for them to be removed. It doesn't take very long to do that, and it will clean up your report for future inquires.

31.     Nationwide. That's the insurance carrier for the subject's home. When a second mortgage was placed on the house, they had the right to check a credit report. People who take out second mortgages on their home may be having financial problems and, over the years, statistics show that people in financial trouble tend to file more insurance claims. The insurance carrier is just checking the credit report to see if they have any credit problems with some of their other lenders. This is usually an indication that they are in financial trouble. By looking at the report at that time, they saw that he was current on all his bills. He spoke to the insurance company and they said there was no problem. Since no problems were detect- ed, the company continued coverage.

32.     That's just another stamp for the consumer copy of the credit file. As noted earlier, that stamp goes on each page sent out.

## Page 3 of Report

33.     Florida National Bank. You'll notice that the date says 11/27/85. We haven't checked the report since this last report and noticed that these were on it. They should be off the next time we check his credit. If they're not, then we'll ask that they be taken off. We may just wait a few more months so that several more are removed as well. You'll notice that there are some inquiries that don't have names. It's very easy to find out who they are, by writing to the credit bureau and asking them to identify the name, address and telephone number of the people who are encoded on the report. If you want to find out who they are, just write to them.

## Page 4 of Report

34.     Consumer Statement on File. The subject gave a Consumer Statement in less than 100 words, because it was a very simple statement. Just above, you'll see where it says #34. It says account closed, reason unknown. This refers to the Chemical account that is right above the one with the $500 credit limit. That was a checking account in New York. He

was conducting business using that account for several years after he came to Florida, but then stopped using it. After about a year of not using that account, a service charge of $8 to $12 was being charged. That added up to well over $100 a year just to keep an inactive account open for a $500 credit line. Our guy wrote a letter to the Chemical Bank requesting that they close the account and transfer that $500 credit limit to either MasterCard or Visa. That's exactly what they did. They increased the Visa card by the $500 credit limit, and they closed this account. It showed up as "account closed; reason unknown." Since it said, "reason unknown," he didn't like the way that read, so he wrote to CBI and asked them to add this consumer statement to his file. What it says is very simple; the date that it's recorded, 10/87, the date to remove it is 10/93. If you want to know something, it's very important that you pick up the phone, call someone, and get the answer. If you're not satisfied with the answer, or you're not sure, don't take everything they say as 100 percent accurate and true. Everybody makes mistakes, or they don't know everything that there is to know.

The step-by-step information that we have just gone over should clarify the information included in a CBI report along with the explanation of "trade line." Study this information until you become familiar with it. We have also included the entire CBI Equifax sheet that they send. Read through it. One important point on the CBI Equifax front page: where it says "Dear Consumer" we put a number 35.

35.     This paragraph reads: "Please remember, the integrity of the consumer credit system demands that credit bureaus maintain and report factual credit history information. This responsibility is shared equally by credit bureaus and credit grantors. Therefore, as mentioned above, if you continue to disagree with any information, you may place a statement of dispute in your record. However, please do not ask CBI or credit grantors to change or delete any information which is correctly recorded." They put

that in there so you do not continuously dispute information that is accurate. They ask that you leave it there. This, however, is a gray area and can often be negotiated. If something from several years ago is being reported as a negative, you have several options for trying to remove it. You could add a consumer statement. You can explain it in a separate letter to a credit grantor. You can go back to that person or credit grantor and try to work something out. Or you can dispute it. If it is a charge-off – a debt you didn't or couldn't pay at the time but now would like to – you can go to that credit grantor and negotiate a way to pay off the debt. Then ask the grantor to send that information to the credit bureau. If you want to start getting yourself on the right track financially, you need to show everyone that you are straightening these things out. This is not an overnight or quick-fix solution. It takes sometimes as long as six months to a year or more to straighten out bad credit. Just remember: The sooner you start, the sooner you'll have it done.

# CBI
# EQUIFAX

Date _____

Dear Consumer:

Enclosed is a copy of the information you requested concerning your credit history contained in CBI's files and the information necessary to fully understand its contents.

The identification information section is self explanatory. The other sections of the report are coded, except for the firm names which are printed next to the information they have reported.

The trade section of the report contains account information. Since much of the account information is coded on the report, an explanation of this information is provided on the inside page.

Inquiries refer to those businesses that have requested and received information concerning your credit history from CBI. They are listed with the date of the request.

Also listed on the inside page are the names of any sources of public records and other information such as bankruptcies, garnishments, judgments, or accounts placed for collection that may not be decoded on the report.

Please review the enclosed information carefully. If you disagree with any information which has been reported to CBI, please complete the enclosed "Consumer Dispute Form", and mail it to us. Upon receipt of this form, we will contact the source of information in dispute, and recheck the information to determine the current status of the account.

After we have contacted the source and obtained the current status, we will update the report accordingly to reflect any new information. When you receive the results of the re-check, please review the updated information carefully to determine if further handling is desirable.

If the information you disagreed with has been changed to reflect a new status, you may request that an amended report be sent to businesses who have requested and received information concerning your credit history in the past six months. If the results of the update indicate that the source continues to report the information that you disagree with, you have the right to submit a personal statement. You may request that the statement of dispute, or summary thereof, be sent to businesses which have received information concerning your credit history in the past six months.

35

Please remember, the integrity of the consumer credit system demands that credit bureaus maintain and report factual credit history information. This responsibility is shared equally by credit bureaus and credit grantors. Therefore, as mentioned above, if you continue to disagree with any information, you may place a statement of dispute in your record. **However, please do not ask CBI or credit grantors to change or delete any information which is correctly recorded.**

Procedures for sending updated reports and consumer statements will be discussed in further detail when we notify you of the results of our re-check. Following these procedures will assure our prompt handling of your request. Thank you for your assistance.

Sincerely,

_____

Consumer Affairs Department

*The Credit Bureau Inc • an Equifax Company*

Systems In Action

# EXPLANATION OF TRADE LINE

THE INFORMATION ON THE REPORT IS SET IN COLUMNS AND BELOW ARE THE DESCRIPTIONS OF THE INFORMATION CONTAINED IN THE COLUMNS.

| FIRM/ID CODE | RPTD | OPND | H/C | TRMS | BAL | P/D | CS | MR | ECOA | ACCOUNT NUMBER |
|---|---|---|---|---|---|---|---|---|---|---|
| 30/60/90 | PREV | HI | RATES | | | | | | | DLA |

**FIRM/ID CODE:** The first item identifies the business that is reporting the information. A name and a number are normally used.

**30/60/90:** The number in the ( ) indicates the number of payments that were received more than 30 days from the date due, ( ) 60 days from the date due, ( ) and 90 days from the date due.

**RPTD:** The date (month/year) the information was reported to CBI. All of the other information shown about this account is as of this date.

**PREV:** 

**OPND:** Up to three (3) dates and manners of payments may appear in this position. They represent the date and manners of payment which were paid other than as agreed.

**HI:** 

**H/C:** This is the month and year you opened the account with the credit grantor.

**RATES:** The highest amount charged or the credit limit is shown in this column.

**TRMS:** This is the terms of the account which was contractually agreed to and may be represented as an amount due per month or the number of months.

**BAL:** 

**P/D:** This figure indicates the amount past due, if any, at the time the information was reported to CBI. The amount owed on the account at the time it was reported to CBI.

**CS:** Current status is shown as a letter indicating the type of account and a number indicating current manner of payment. See Explanation of Coded Information below.

**MR:** This indicates the number of times the account has been reviewed or reported to CBI.

**ECOA:** This is the Equal Credit Opportunity Act account designator and identifies the type of participation on the account. See Explanation of Coded Information below.

**ACCOUNT NUMBER:** This is your account number with the company reporting.

**DLA:** This is the date of last activity on the account and may be the date of last payment or the date of last charge to the credit grantor.

# EXPLANATION OF CODED INFORMATION

## E C O A

The Equal Credit Opportunity Act designators explain who is responsible for the account and the type of participation you have with the account.

J — Joint
I — Individual
U — Undesignated
A — Authorized user
T — Terminated
M — Maker
C — Co-Maker

B — On Behalf of another person
S — Shared

* an asterisk designates this information is reported to CBI on a Regular Basis.

**TERMS OF SALE**

Open Account (30 days or 90 days) ............................O
Revolving or Option (Open-end account) ........................R
Installment (fixed number of payments) .........................I

| CURRENT MANNER OF PAYMENT | TYPE ACCOUNT | | |
|---|---|---|---|
| | O | R | I |
| Too new to rate; approved but not used | 0 | 0 | |
| Pays (or paid) within 30 days, of billing; pays account as agreed | 1 | 1 | 1 |
| Pays (or paid) in more than 30 days, but not more than 60 days, or not more than one payment past due | 2 | 2 | 2 |
| Pays (or paid) in more than 60 days, but not more than 90 days, or two payments past due | 3 | 3 | 3 |
| Pays (or paid) in more than 90 days, but not more than 120 days, or three or more payments past due | 4 | 4 | 4 |
| Pays (or paid) in more than 120 days | 5 | 5 | 5 |
| Making regular payments under wage earner plan or similar arrangements | 7 | 7 | 7 |
| Repossession | 8 | 8 | 8 |
| Bad debt; placed for collection | 9 | 9 | 9 |

## Public Record And Other Information

In some instances the source reporting and other details of a transaction appear in coded form. Listed below are those sources of other information that are not decoded on the report including any necessary explanation

| Item | Code Number | Source/Description |
|---|---|---|
| | | |
| | | |
| | | |
| | | |
| | | |
| | | |

# CONSUMER DISPUTE FORM

_____ _____
Area Code         Telephone No.

## _Personal Identification_ _(Please Print or Type)_

Name_____
(Last)                          (First)                    (Middle Initial)              Suffix (Jr., Sr., etc.)

Present Address _____
(Street)                        (City)                     (State)                      (Zip)

Former Address _____
(Street)                        (City)                     (State)                      (Zip)

Date of Birth _____  Social Security Number _____
(Month)      (Day)      (Year)

I RECENTLY RECEIVED A COPY OF THE REPORT CONTAINING MY CREDIT HISTORY, AND I DISAGREE WITH THE FOLLOWING INFORMATION:

## CREDIT HISTORY

| Name of Business | Account Number | Specific nature of disagreement |
|---|---|---|
|  |  |  |
|  |  |  |
|  |  |  |
|  |  |  |
|  |  |  |
|  |  |  |
|  |  |  |

| Public Record And Other Information Court or Business | Case Number | Nature of disagreement |
|---|---|---|
|  |  |  |
|  |  |  |

| Other: (i.e. information from other credit bureaus, etc.) | Item | Nature of disagreement |
|---|---|---|
|  |  |  |
|  |  |  |

I understand that the information I have disputed will be rechecked when necessary at the source, and I will be notified of the results of this recheck.

_____     _____
(Signature)                                        (Date)

71

# WHAT YOU SHOULD KNOW ABOUT THE CREDIT BUREAU, INC.
## AND
## THE LAW GOVERNING CREDIT BUREAUS

## OUR PURPOSE:

Our purpose at the Credit Bureau, Inc. (CBI) is to serve the community by providing businesses the information they need to properly grant credit to consumers.

## WHAT IS IN THE CREDIT FILE:

The information maintained by CBI to assist credit grantors in their processing of credit applications typically includes such facts as your name, address, birthdate, job, present and previous employers, the manner in which you have paid your bills (as reported by your creditors), and whether you have filed for bankruptcy, or had a tax lien or judgment recorded against you.

CBI furnishes this information to individual business firms, who then make the actual decision of whether, under their own policies, they will grant you credit. CBI does not rate your credit or recommend that your credit application be accepted or rejected. Each credit grantor decides that on the basis of many factors, such as total income, the amount of credit applied for, and the effect it will have on your total indebtedness.

## THE FAIR CREDIT REPORTING ACT:

The Federal Fair Credit Reporting Act (FCRA) became law on April 25, 1971. It assures you of certain rights concerning information about you.

The Fair Credit Reporting Act Provides that:

1. You must be told by the user of the report the name and address of the credit bureau responsible for preparing a report that was used, in whole or in part, to deny you a benefit, or to increase the cost of a benefit.
2. At your request, you must be told by a credit bureau the nature, substance, and names of sources of information collected about you.
3. Unfavorable information, in most cases, may not be reported after seven years. One major exception is bankruptcy, which may be reported for ten years.
4. If you dispute information in the file, any necessary reinvestigation will be made. If the credit bureau cannot confirm the information, it will be removed from the file, and a corrected report will be sent to those you specify who have received a report within the past six months (for employment purposes, within the past two years).
5. If the credit bureau reconfirms the information with which you disagree, you may write a statement telling your side of the story. Your statement will be sent, at your request, to anyone who has received a report within the past six months (for employment purposes, within the past two years). Your statement, or summary of it, will also be made available with any future reports that contain the disputed information.

CBI CRC SARASOTA
1960 LANDINGS BLVD ,STE 207
P.O. BOX 4008
SARASOTA, FL. 34230

ACB OF A = 20294

| DATE RECEIVED | DATE MAILED | |
|---|---|---|
| 11/09/87 | 11/09/87 | |
| DATE TRADE CLEARED | DATE EMPL. VERIFIED | INCOME VERIFIED |
| RE:D/RPTD | | YES  X  NO |

**CBI** Systems in Action
Mortgage Reporting Division

| FOR **1** | IN FILE SINCE |
|---|---|
| 835AA00055,J,REVISED COPY,AU6 | |
| INQUIRED AS | 12/28/81 |
| VAIRO,DOUGLAS,A | |

| REPORT ON (SURNAME) | SOCIAL SECURITY NUMBER | SPOUSE'S NAME |
|---|---|---|
| VAIRO,DOUGLAS,A, | | |
| ADC | RESIDENCE SINCE | SPOUSE'S SOC. SEC. NO. |
| | | CRT RPTD 05/8 |

| PRESENT EMPLOYER | POSITION HELD | MONTHLY INC. | SINCE |
|---|---|---|---|
| V M CARD CORNER,PUNT,FL | VARIETY VIDEOS | 5000 | |

| DATE OF BIRTH | NUMBER OF DEPENDENTS | | X | OWNS | BUYING | RENTS |
|---|---|---|---|---|---|---|
| AGE 32 | | | | | | |
| FORMER ADDRESS | | | **2** | FROM | TO | |
| PORT CHARLOTTE,FL,33948,CRT RPTD 10/87 | | | | | | |
| FORMER EMPLOYER | POSITION HELD | MONTHLY INC. | FROM | TO | | |

| **3** FIRM IDENTIFICATION CODE | **4** DATE RPTD | **5** DATE OPND | **6** H/C | **7** T R_M | **8** B_AL | **9** P/D | **10** C_S | **11** M_R | **12** E C O A | **13** ACCOUNT NUMBER |
|---|---|---|---|---|---|---|---|---|---|---|
| **14** CHEMICAL  426BB1648 | 11/87 | 01/82 | 3100 | 128 | 2747 | | R1 | I | | 4114206 |
| | | | | | | | | | **15** | DLA 08/87 |
| CHEMICAL  426BB1648 | 11/87 | 04/92 | 500 | 21 | 407 | | R1 | I | | 5263000204 |
| | | | | | | | | | | DLA 08/87 |
| FREEDOM  *4470N119 | 09/87 | 06/85 | 2300 | | 2132 | | R1 | 26 | I | 3001 |
| | | | | | | | | | | DLA 09/87 |
| **16** AMOUNT IN H/C COLUMN IS CREDIT LIMIT | | | | | | | | | | |
| 1ST SELECT*162FZ938 | 09/87 | 07/85 | 3241 | 60 | 3004 | | R1 | 26 | I **17** | 423323072 |
| | | | | | | | | | | DLA 09/87 |
| J C PENNEY*906DC185 | 09/87 | 12/83 | 619 | 40 | 305 | | R1 | 43 | S | 21-21803 |
| | | | | | | | | | | DLA 09/87 |
| **18** BARNETT BK 835BB128 | 10/87 | 05/85 | 30K | | 0 | 0 | I1 | | I | 04-6291 |
| | | | | | | | | | | DLA 06/86 |
| BARNETT BK 835BB128 | 10/87 | 06/86 | 20K | 396 | 6069 | 0 | I1 | | I | 04-6291 |
| FIRSTFLABK*7280N135 | 09/87 | 08/85 | 1037 | | 837 | | R1 | 12 | I | 367006025 |
| | | | | | | | | | | DLA 09/87 |
| **19** AVCO FIN  *425FZ33 | 09/87 | 08/85 | 2193 | 36M | 718 | | I1 | 02 | I | 206-516 |
| | | | | | | | | | | DLA 09/87 |
| MARINE MID*405BB280 | 09/87 | 12/85 | 5000 | | 3877 | | R1 | 12 | I | 165 |
| AMOUNT IN H/C COLUMN IS CREDIT LIMIT | | | | | | | | | | |
| 1ST FL BK *835BB177 | 09/87 | 09/85 | 5054 | | 4646 | | R1 | 12 | I | 16200 |
| | | | | | | | | | | DLA 09/87 |
| ROBINSON'S*906DC86 | 08/87 | 02/85 | 0 | | 0 | | R1 | 29 | I | 85 |
| | | | | | | | | | | DLA 02/85 |
| CHEMICAL  *426BB1648 | 08/87 | 12/81 | 5000 | 112 | 2639 | | R1 | 64 | I | 5263000204 |
| | | | | | | | | | | DLA 08/87 |

FN 44-0040397-01-300

PAGE 1

REMARKS
Credit History
A The reporting agency certifies the subject's credit history in the payment of obligations has been updated based on availability of information and local conditions.
B The absence of 30 60 90 day counters indicates zero late notices.
Public Record
Through systematic filing, independent research, and appropriate sources public record information on the subject has been checked at all known addresses for a period of seven years.

F100

```
CBI CRC SARASOTA
1960 LANDINGS BLVD ,STE 207
P.O. BOX 4008
SARASOTA, FL. 34230

ACB OF A = 20294
```

| DATE RECEIVED | DATE MAILED | |
|---|---|---|
| 11/09/87 | 11/09/87 | |
| DATE TRADE CLEARED | DATE EMPL. VERIFIED | INCOME VERIFIED |
| RE:D/RPTD | | YES  X  NC |

**CBI** Systems in Action
**Mortgage Reporting Division**

FOR
835AA00055,J;REVISED COPY,AU6

INQUIRED AS
VAIRO,DOUGLAS,A

| IN FILE SINCE |
|---|
| 12/28/81 |

| REPORT ON (SURNAME) | SOCIAL SECURITY NUMBER | SPOUSE'S NAME |
|---|---|---|
| VAIRO,DOUGLAS,A, | | |

| ADDRESS | RESIDENCE SINCE | SPOUSE'S SOC. SEC. NO. |
|---|---|---|
| PORT CHARLOTTE,FL,33948 | | CRT RPTD 05/8 |

| PRESENT EMPLOYER | POSITION HELD | MONTHLY INC. | SINCE |
|---|---|---|---|
| | | | |

| DATE OF BIRTH | NUMBER OF DEPENDENTS | | OWNS | BUYING | | RENTS |
|---|---|---|---|---|---|---|
| | | | | | | |

| FORMER ADDRESS | | FROM | TO |
|---|---|---|---|
| | | | |

| FORMER EMPLOYER | POSITION HELD | MONTHLY INC. | FROM | TO |
|---|---|---|---|---|
| | | | | |

| | FIRM IDENTIFICATION CODE | DATE RPTD | DATE OPND | H/C | $T_{RM}$ | $B_{AL}$ | P/D | $C_S$ | $M_R$ | ECOA | ACCOUNT NUMBER |
|---|---|---|---|---|---|---|---|---|---|---|---|
| | AMOUNT IN H/C COLUMN IS CREDIT LIMIT | | | | | | | | | | |
| 21 | BK1-COL-VI*1480N28 | 08/87 | 02/87 | 30 | | 0 | | R1 | 05 | I | 43879 |
| | | | | | | | | | | | DLA 04/87 |
| 22 | AVCO  *906FP509 | 07/87 | 08/85 | 2193 | 36M | 0 | | I1 | 22 | I | 26-88 |
| | | | | | | | | | | | DLA 07/87 |
| 23 | ACCOUNT TRANSFERRED | | | | | | | | | | |
| 24 | SEARS  *906DC29 | 04/87 | 02/87 | 42 | | 43 | | R1 | 01 | I | 8655-75971 |
| | RHODES FUR*402HF310 | 11/86 | 11/83 | 1429 | 64 | 0 | 0 | R1 | 34 | U | 35-045 |
| | | | | | | | | | | | DLA 12/85 |
| | 1ST FL BK *835BB177 | 10/85 | 02/84 | 2387 | 24M | 0 | | I1 | 19 | I | 1601010 |
| | | | | | | | | | | | DLA 08/85 |
| | AVCO FIN  *425FZ33 | 08/85 | 05/85 | 2084 | 36M | 0 | | I1 | 02 | I | 206-380 |
| | | | | | | | | | | | DLA 08/85 |
| 25 | EASTERN  *401ZS321 | 08/85 | 08/85 | 1000 | | 0 | | RO | | I | 2007307 |
| | | | | | | | | | | | DLA 08/85 |
| | AMOUNT IN H/C COLUMN IS CREDIT LIMIT | | | | | | | | | | |
| | CHEM IL  *426BB3024 | 05/84 | 11/81 | 2715 | 75 | 0 | | I1 | 27 | I | 2930000 |
| | | | | | | | | | | | DLA 05/84 |

```
26   SD LEASING/LITTLE ROCK/AR, 12/86,OP-04/84,I1,H/C-1949,BAL-0,DLA-04/86
     MANUF HANOVER TRUST, 06/81,OP-02/78,I1,H/C-1500,BAL-0,DLA-06/81

*    NO PUBLIC RECORDS OR OTHER INFORMATION IN FILE
27  *INQS-SUBJECT SHOWS  7 INQUIRIES SINCE 08/87
        28 CONS SVC    835AA55    11/09/87    CONS SVC    835AA55    10/22/87
           OPTIMAAECB 1900N143   10/21/87  29 CONS COPY   835AA22    10/07/87
        30 PRM 905BB00033        08/24/87  31 NATIONWIDE 728IG184    09/23/87
                           32 Consumer Copy Of Credit File
                              Not To Be Used As A Credit Report
```

```
FN 44-0040397-01-300                                              PAGE
```

REMARKS
Credit History
A. The reporting agency certifies the subject's credit history in the payment of obligations has been updated based on availability of information and local conditions.
B. The absence of 30, 60, 90 day counters indicates zero late notices.
Public Record.
Through systematic filing, independent research, and appropriate sources public record information on the subject has been checked at all known addresses for a period of seven years.

F100

CBI CRC SARASOTA
1960 LANDINGS BLVD , STE 207
P.O. BOX 4003
SARASOTA, FL. 34230

ACB OF A = 20294

| DATE RECEIVED | DATE MAILED | |
|---|---|---|
| 11/09/87 | 11/09/87 | |
| DATE TRADE CLEARED | DATE EMPL. VERIFIED | INCOME VERIFIED |
| RE:D/RPTD | | YES  X  NO |

## CBI  Systems in Action
### Mortgage Reporting Division

| FOR | IN FILE SINCE |
|---|---|
| 835AA00055,J,REVISED COPY,AU6 | |
| INQUIRED AS | 12/28/81 |
| VAIRO,DOUGLAS,A | |

| REPORT ON (SURNAME) | SOCIAL SECURITY NUMBER | SPOUSE'S NAME |
|---|---|---|
| VAIRO,DOUGLAS,A, | | |

| ADDRESS | RESIDENCE SINCE | SPOUSE'S SOC. SEC. NO. |
|---|---|---|
| ,PORT CHARLOTTE,FL,33948 | | CRT RPTD 05/ |

| PRESENT EMPLOYER | POSITION HELD | MONTHLY INC. | SINCE |
|---|---|---|---|
| | | | |

| DATE OF BIRTH | NUMBER OF DEPENDENTS | OWNS | BUYING | RENTS |
|---|---|---|---|---|
| | | | | |

| FORMER ADDRESS | FROM | TO |
|---|---|---|
| | | |

| FORMER EMPLOYER | POSITION HELD | MONTHLY INC. | FROM | TO |
|---|---|---|---|---|
| | | | | |

| | FIRM IDENTIFICATION CODE | DATE RPTD | DATE OPND | H/C | $T_{R_M}$ | $B_{A_L}$ | P/D | $C_S$ | $M_R$ | ECOA | ACCOUNT NUMBER | | |
|---|---|---|---|---|---|---|---|---|---|---|---|---|---|
| | BARNETT BK 835BB128 | 09/03/87 | | | | CHEMICAL | | 426BB1648 | | | | 05/06/87 | |
| | PRM 906BB00115 | 04/17/87 | | | | 1ST FL BK | | 835BB177 | | | | 01/28/87 | |
| | BANK ONE 905BB4332 | 01/10/87 | | | | TELTEC | | 402UT1039 | | | | 12/03/86 | |
| | CONS SVC 835AA55 | 11/12/86 | | | | CONS COPY | | 835AA22 | | | | 11/10/86 | |
| | 9050N1331 | 06/25/86 | | | | | | 835FP215 | | | | 06/18/86 | |
| | BARNETT BK 835BB128 | 06/11/86 | | | | C&S PTCH | | 835BB1133 | | | | 05/23/86 | |
| | CONS COPY 835AA22 | 02/07/86 | | | | | | 826BB1341 | | | | 12/13/85 | |
| 33 | FLA NAT BK 826BB21045 | 11/27/85 | | | | MAR MID MC | | 405BB2161 | | | | 11/26/85 | |
| | DINERS 9050N93 | 11/26/85 | | | | SUN BANK | | 4470N85 | | | | 11/14/85 | |
| | C & S BANK 4470N408 | 11/13/85 | | | | | | | | | | | |

Computer ... ... ...
Not To Be ...

FN 44-0040397-01-300

COMPLETE   PAGE

REMARKS
Credit History
A The reporting agency certifies the subject's credit history in the payment of obligations has been updated based on availability of information and local conditions.
B The absence of 30, 60, 90 day counters indicates zero late notices.
Public Record
Through systematic long, independent research, and appropriate sources public record information on the subject has been checked at all known addresses for a period of seven years.

F100

RESTART 035

CBI CRC SARASOTA
1960 LANDINGS BLVD ,STE 207
P.O. BOX 4008
SARASOTA, FL. 34230

ACB OF A = 20294

| | | |
|---|---|---|
| DATE RECEIVED | DATE MAILED | |
| 10/22/87 | 10/22/87 | INCOME VERIFIED |
| DATE TRADE CLEARED | DATE EMPL. VERIFIED | YES  X  NO |
| RE:D/RPTD | | |

**CBI** Systems in Action
Mortgage Reporting Division

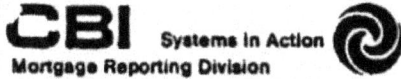

FOR  835AA00055,J,REVISED COPY,AUG
INQUIRED AS  VAIRO,DOUGLAS,A

IN FILE SINCE  12/28/81

| REPORT ON (SURNAME) | SOCIAL SECURITY NUMBER | SPOUSE'S NAME |
|---|---|---|
| VAIRO,DOUGLAS,A, | | |

| ADDRESS | RESIDENCE SINCE | SPOUSE'S SOC SEC. NO |
|---|---|---|
| 102,ROCK CREEK,DR,PORT CHARLOTTE,FL,33948 | | CRT RPTD 05/9? |

| PRESENT EMPLOYER | POSITION HELD | MONTHLY INC | SINCE |
|---|---|---|---|

| DATE OF BIRTH | NUMBER OF DEPENDENTS | OWNS | BUYING | RENTS |
|---|---|---|---|---|

| FORMER ADDRESS | | FROM | TO |
|---|---|---|---|

| FORMER EMPLOYER | POSITION HELD | MONTHLY INC | FROM | TO |
|---|---|---|---|---|

| FIRM IDENTIFICATION CODE | DATE RPTD | DATE OPND | H/C | T$_{RM}$ | B$_{AL}$ | P/D | C$_S$ | M$_R$ | ECOA | ACCOUNT NUMBER |
|---|---|---|---|---|---|---|---|---|---|---|
| 34 CONSUMER STATEMENT ON FILE WITH: | | | | | | | | | | |
| CBI CRC SARASOTA 1960 LANDINGS BLVD ,STE 207 P.O. BOX 4008 SARASOTA, FL. 34230 | | | | | | | | | | |

DATE RECORDED  10/87     DATE TO REMOVE  10/93
(ITEM CLOSED ACCOUNT CHEMICAL BANK) ACCOUNT CLOSED PER MY REQUEST,CHECKING ACC
OUNT WITH OVERDRAFT,NO LONGER USED CHECKING ACCOUNT AND ASKED TO CLOSE ACCOUNT

| | | | | | | | | | | |
|---|---|---|---|---|---|---|---|---|---|---|
| 1ST SELEC #162F2938 | 08/87 | 07/85 | 5241 | 67 | 2827 | | R1 | 25 | I | 4233230 DLA 07/87 |
| CHEMICAL #416BB1648 | 08/87 | 04/82 | 500 | 21 | 480 | | R1 | 00 | I | 5263000 DLA 08/87 |
| 34 ACCOUNT CLOSED - REASON UNKNOWN | | | | | | | | | | |

Not To Be Used As A Credit Report

FN 44-0001670-02-300

PAGE 1

F100

Consumer Copy, ...
Not To Be Used As A Credit Report

FN 44-0001670-02-300

PAGE 3

F100

76

THE CREDIT BUREAU INC
REGIONAL CENTER
2705 N.E. 183RD ST

MIAMI FL 33160

| | IN FILE | | SINGLE REF. | | TRADE |
| | EV&T | | FULL | | PREV. RES. |

| DATE RECEIVED | DATE MAILED | CBR REPORT |
|---|---|---|
| 01/05/88 | 01/05/88 | |
| DATE TRADE CLEARED | DATE EMPL. VERIFIED | INCOME VERIFIED |
| RESID/RPTD | | YES        NO |

CONFIDENTIAL crediscope® REPORT

Member
Associated Credit Bureaus, Inc.

FOR 402AA00311,J,CONSUMER COPY,BJ9
INQUIRED AS

IN FILE SINCE:
11/20/37.

REPORT ON (SURNAME):

SOCIAL SECURITY NUMBER:

SPOUSE'S NAME:

ADDRESS: ,CAPE CORAL,FL,33910

| STATE: | ZIP CODE | RESIDENCE SINCE: |
|---|---|---|

DAT RPTD 11/8

PRESENT EMPLOYER | POSITION HELD: | MONTHLY INC. SINCE

DATE OF BIRTH | NUMBER OF DEPENDENTS | | OWNS | | RENTS

FORMER ADDRESS | CITY: | STATE: | FROM: | TO:

FORMER EMPLOYER | POSITION HELD. | MONTHLY INC. FROM: | TO:

OTHER'S EMPLOYER | DATE VERIFIED | POSITION HELD | MONTHLY INC. FROM: | TO:

NOT FOR CONSUMER REVIEW COPY NOT FOR CREDIT GRANTING PURPOSES

## CREDIT HISTORY

| FIRM/ID CODE | RPTD | OPND | H/C | TRM | BAL | P/D | CS | MR | ECOA | ACCOUNT NUMBER |
|---|---|---|---|---|---|---|---|---|---|---|
| FIRST CARD #765BB33 | 10/87 ACCOUNT INCLUDED IN BANKRUPTCY | | | | | | | | | 4673631406120 DLA 09/87 |

AMOUNT IN H/C COLUMN IS CREDIT LIMIT

NO PUBLIC RECORDS OR OTHER INFORMATION IN FILE
INQUIRIES-CONSU MAIL 402AA344    01/05/88    AMER C B    402YC1667    11/20/87

**Trans Union Credit Information Co.**
**New York Division**

95-25 Queens Boulevard
Rego Park, N.Y. 11374
212/459-1800

Consumer Relations Department

```
                                          ┐


                                          ┘
```

Dear Consumer:

6-28-83

We enclose a copy of your credit profile, as requested by you.
If you dispute the accuracy of any item in the enclosed report, please
notify us in writing immediately so that we may re-investigate the
item involved.  If the dispute cannot be readily resolved and you
furnish us with your version of the facts, we shall place your statement
in your file and it will be included in all future credit reports.

Please note that we do not rate or evaluate the credit standing of any
consumer.  All credit reports or profiles are merely factual
compilations of credit history.  The decision to grant or withhold
credit is made solely be the credit grantor, i.e. the store, the bank,
etc., not by us.

You may be assured of our willingness to cooperate with you and
assist you in every way possible.


Very truly yours,


Consumer Relations Department


encl. - Buyers' Guide of Federal Trade Commission
        Consumer's Credit Profile


CR-4

# CONSUMER'S BILL OF RIGHTS

If you have been denied credit because of incorrect or incomplete information contained in a report furnished by a Consumer Reporting Agency, the law grants you certain rights, including the following:

1. The right to request in writing and to obtain from the Agency, upon proper identification of the Consumer, the nature and substance of all information (except medical information) contained in the Agency's files at the time of the request.

2. The right to request in writing and to obtain from the Agency, upon proper identification of the Consumer, the sources of all information (except investigative reports).

3. The name and address of all recipients of an adverse report concerning the Consumer given within six months of the date of the request, or within two years of the request if the report was given for employment purposes.

4. The right to dispute in writing the information contained in an adverse report about the Consumer, and the right to have the Consumer's version of the dispute placed in the Agency's file and included in future consumer reports.

5. The right to request in writing that adverse information believed by the Consumer to be incorrect or incomplete, be reinvestigated by the Agency (unless the request is frivolous), and if the information is then found to be incorrect, or if it

cannot be verified, the right to have the Agency remove such information from the Consumer's file.

6. The right to request in writing and to obtain from the Agency a copy of all information to which the Consumer is entitled, without charge, in cases where the Consumer has been denied credit, insurance or employment, within thirty days of the Consumer's interview. Otherwise, the Agency is permitted to charge a reasonable fee for giving t#e Consumer this information.

7. The right to request the Agency in writing that it notify (without charge) those named by the Consumer who previously received the incorrect or incomplete information that such information has been deleted from the Consumer's file.

8. The right to request the Agency in writing to send the Consumer's version of the dispute to certain companies for a reasonable fee.

9. The right to have the Agency withhold a Consumer's report from any one who under the law does not have a legitimate need for the information.

10. The right not to have adverse information reported by the Agency after seven years (except for bankruptcy, which is ten years).

- - - - - - - - - -

# A Guide To Reading The
# Focus Form 2000
## People In Focus

**Trans Union Credit Information Co.**

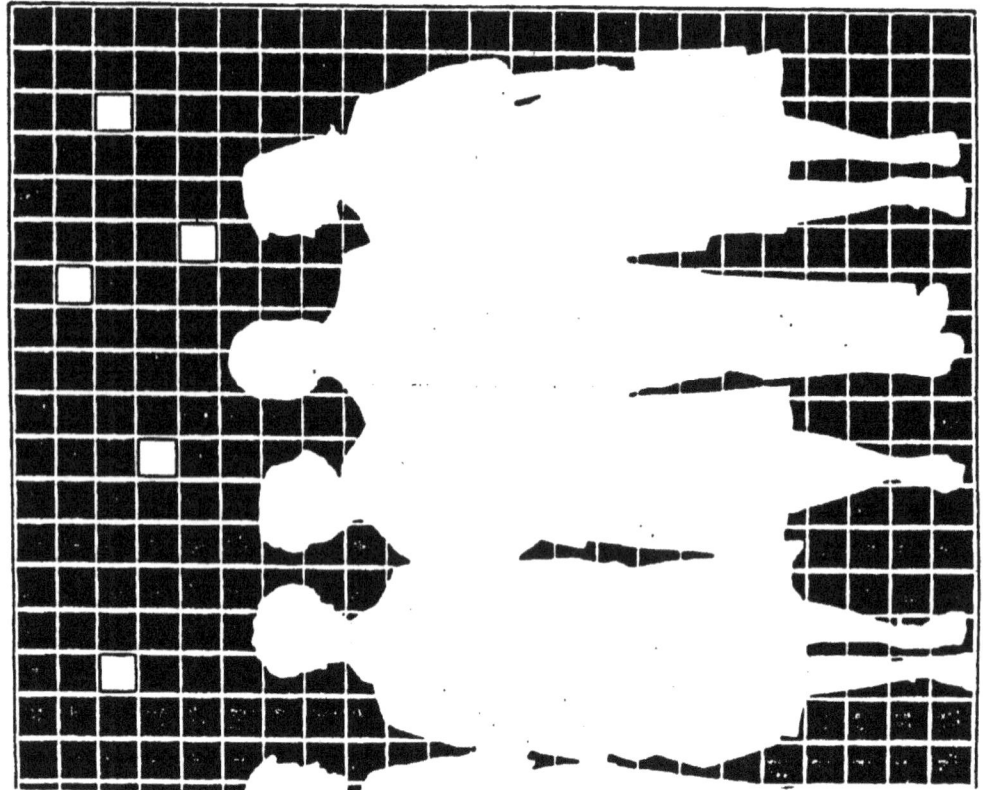

## FOCUS FORM 2000 CODES

### ECOA INQUIRY AND ACCOUNT DESIGNATORS

I  Individual account for sole use of applicant
C  Joint contractual liability
A  Authorized user of shared account

P  Participant in shared account which cannot be distinguished as C or A
3  Co-signer no spouse relationship
M  Co-signer primarily liable for account

T  Relationship with account terminated
U  Undesignated
N  Non-applicant spouse inquiry

### REMARKS AND DISPUTE CODES

AIP  Adjustment pending
BKL  Bankruptcy loss
CCA  Consumer counseling account
CLA  Placed for collection
CLO  Closed to further purchases by either set or or credit
CTS  Contact subscriber
DIS  Dispute following resolution
DRP  Dispute resolution pending
FCL  Foreclosure
JUD  Judgement obtained
MOV  Moved, left no forwarding address
PPL  Profit and loss write-off
RIN  Reinstated account

RLD  Repossession, paid by dealer
RLP  Repossession, proceeds applied to debt
RPO  Repossession, redeemed
RRE  Repossession, redeemed
RS   Dispute resolved
RVD  Returned voluntarily, paid by dealer
RVR  Returned voluntarily, proceeds applied to debt
RVR  Returned voluntarily, redeemed
SET  Settled for less than full balance
STL  Plate stolen or lost
TRF  Transferred account
WEP  Wage Earner Plan Account (Chapter XIII)

### PUBLIC RECORD TYPES

AG  Annulment Granted
AN  Annulment
AT  Chapter 13 Adjudicated
AQ  Acquitted
BD  Bankruptcy Dismissed
BR  Bankruptcy
CB  Civil Judgement in Bankruptcy
CD  Civil Suit Disputed
CO  Civil Judgement Disputed
CM  Chattel Mortgage
CJ  Civil Judgement
CS  Change of Name
CS  Civil Suit Filed
DB  Discharged Bankruptcy
DD  Judgement for Defendant
DE  Deed and Mortgage
DF  Dismissed Foreclosure
DG  Divorce Granted
DJ  Delinquency Judgement
DM  Deeds and Mortgage (NY PHIL)
DM  Divorce Dismissed
DS  Dismissal of Court Suit
DT  Chapter 13 Dismissed
DV  Divorce
FC  Foreclosure
FD  Forcible Detainer
FR  Foreclosure Real Estate Sold
FS  Financing Statement
FT  Federal Tax Lien
GN  Garnishment
HS  Homestead
JC  Judgement by Confession
JD  Judgement by Default
JM  Dismissed Judgement
LP  Lis Pendens
LT  Landlord Tenant
MC  Miscellaneous
ML  Mechanics Lien
ND  Notice of Default
NJ  Attachment, no Judgement
NR  Notice Non Responsible
PC  Paid Civil Judgement
PD  Petition for Dissolution
PF  Paid Federal Tax Lien
PL  Release of State Tax Lien (CA)
PS  Paid Tax Lien
PS  Public Sale
PV  Judgement Paid, Vacated
RA  Real Estate Attachment
RL  Release Tax Lien
RM  Release Mechanics Lien
RN  Release Non Responsible
RP  Reprmnt
RS  Real Estate Attach Satisfied
RW  Paid Civil Judgement
SF  Satisfied Foreclosure
SQ  Separate Bill of Maintenance Granted
SH  Sheriffs Sale
SL  State Tax Lien
SM  Separate Bill of Maintenance
SP  Separation
SS  Satisfied Civil Suit
ST  Chapter 13 Successful
TC  Trusteeship Cancelled
TD  Trust Deed
TL  Tax Lien Other
TR  Trusteeship
WA  Wage Assignment
WD  Warranty Deeds
11  Chapter 11 Bankruptcy
13  Chapter 13 Bankruptcy

### TYPE OF ACCOUNT

O  Open Account (30, 60 or 90 days)
R  Revolving or Option
I  Installment
M  Mortgage
C  Check credit (line of credit)

### KINDS OF BUSINESS CLASSIFICATION

A  Automotive
B  Banks
C  Clothing
D  Department and Variety
F  Finance
G  Groceries
H  Home Furnishings
I  Insurance
J  Jewelry and Cameras
K  Contractors
L  Lumber Building Material, Hardware
M  Medical and Related Health
N  National Credit Card
O  Oil and National Credit Card Companies
P  Personal Services Other Than Medical
Q  Mail Order Houses
R  Real Estate and Public Accommodations
S  Sporting Goods
T  Farm and Garden Supplies
U  Utilities and Fuel
V  Government
W  Wholesale
X  Advertising
Y  Collection Services
Z  Miscellaneous

### USUAL MANNER OF PAYMENT

| Code | Description |
|------|-------------|
| 00 | Not rated, too new to rate or approved but not used |
| 01 | Pays (or paid) within 30 days of billing, pays accounts as agreed |
| 02 | Pays (or paid) in more than 30 days but not more than 60 days, or not more than one payment past due |
| 03 | Pays (or paid) in more than 60 days but not more than 90 days, or two payments past due |
| 04 | Pays (or paid) in more than 90 days or not more than 120 days, or three or more payments past due |
| 05 | Pays (or paid) in 120 days or more |
| 07 | Makes regular payments under wage earner plan or similar arrangement |
| 08 | Repossession |
| 8A | Voluntary Repossession |
| 8D | Legal Repossession |
| 8R | Repossession redeemed |
| 09 | Bad debt, placed for collection, suit judgment bankrupt, skip |
| 9B | Collection Account |
| UR | Unrated |
| UC | Unclassified |
| RJ | Rejected |

### TYPE OF INSTALLMENT LOAN

AF  Appliance/Furniture
AP  Airplane
AU  Automobile
BT  Boat
CA  Camper
CM  Co-Maker
CO  Consolidation
CS  Conditional Sales Contract
EQ  Equipment
FA  Farm Equipment
FH  FHA Loan
HI  Home Improvement
HW  Hardware and Building Material
IN  Insurance
LE  Leases
MB  Mobile Home
MC  Miscellaneous
MT  Motor Homes
PI  Property
PL  Improvement Plan
PL  Personal Loan
PS  Partly Secured
RE  Real Estate
RV  Recreational Vehicle
ST  Student Loan
SV  Savings Book Stock, Etc
UK  Unknown
US  Unsecured
VA  VA Loan

### COLLECTION STATUS CODES

PD  Paid
UK  Unknown
DM  Dismissed

UP  Unpaid
DP  Disputed
BL  Discharged in Bankruptcy

### PUBLIC RECORD SOURCE

The Public Record Source is displayed as an alpha indicator or a numeric indicator and the City or County court source.

Example 25 Cook County

### COURT CODES

MU  Municipal Court
SC  Superior Court
DO  Domestic Court
FE  Federal District Court
SU  Justice of the Peace
JU  Small Claims
CI  Circuit Court
M1  1st Magisterial Court
CA  County Auditor

M2  2nd Magisterial Court
M3  3rd Magisterial Court
M4  Quarterly Court
CC  County Clerk's Office
CH  Chancery Court
GS  General Session
IC  Inferior Court
PR  Probate Court
DS  District Judge System

### DATE INDICATORS

A  Automated
C  Closed
D  Declined
F  Repossessed/Written Off
I  Indirect
M  Manually Frozen
N  No Record

P  Paid Out
R  Reported but not verified
S  Slow Answering
T  Terminated
V  Verified
X  No Reply

**Trans Union Credit Information Co.**

CONFIDENTIAL

REPORT ON: WINSLOW, DONALD JOHN

1) Your Trans Union Credit Information Co. subscriber inquiry code number
2) How long the consumer has been in the credit bureau files
3) Consumer's last, first and middle name or initial, also alias if any
4) Consumer's social security number
5) Spouse's name
6) Consumer's complete address
7) Trans Union Credit Information Co. market area accessed via your terminal
8) Consumer's social security number
9) Spouse's employer and address
10) Consumer's stock number, position and date hired (H), reported (R), or verified (V) by bureau
11) Consumer's income: Y - yearly, M - monthly, H - hourly, W - weekly, S - semimonthly, B - bimonthly, D - daily
12) Consumer's date of birth or estimated age (E-XX)
13) Number of dependents including spouse
14) Whether the consumer owns, rents or boards
15) Consumer's home phone number
16) Consumer's previous address
17) Dates that consumer resided at that address
18) Second previous address of consumer
19) Dates that consumer resided at that address
20) Previous employer and address
21) Clock number, position and date employment verified
22) Date consumer was hired and terminated at former place of employment
23) Spouse's complete employment, company name and address
24) Name of credit grantor where consumer has credit account
25) Credit grantor's Trans Union Credit Information Co. subscriber code number
26) Date that particular account was opened
27) Responsibility for repaying the debt (i.e., Individual account, joint account, authorized user account, etc.)
28) The high credit on the account. (The highest amount ever owed)
29) The date closed/verified column has a date, and one of the indicators listed below:
   a) A - verified by automated tape
   b) C - date account was closed
   c) F - date account was frozen, due either to repossession or charge-off
   d) M - manually frozen
   e) P - paid out date for an open account with a zero balance not in dispute
   f) V - verified manually
30) Balance owing as of date in closed/verified column
31) Credit Limit: the maximum amount of credit approved by the creditor
32) Amount past due as of date in closed/verified column
33) Number of payments past due as of date in closed/verified column
34) Payment pattern gives you the actual manner of payment ratings 1 through 9, for a maximum of 12 months. It reads from left to right, with the most current verified entry on the left. The pattern then works its way back in time. I an X appears in the payment pattern it means that there was no information or rating available for the month. The first entry corresponds to the date in the date closed/verified column.
35) Type of account: R-revolving, I-installment, O-open; 30 day account, C-check credit, M-mortgage, and the ACB manner of payment rating system
36) The account number of the consumer for a particular grantor
37) The collateral for an installment loan
38) Type of installment loan: auto, boat, personal, airplane, etc.
39) Terms of sale, number of payments, payment frequency and dollar amount due each payment. The codes are: X-unspecified, M-monthly, P-payroll deduction, S-semiannual, Q-quarterly, Y-yearly, W-weekly, B-biweekly
40) Maximum delinquency consists of three columns: the 1st is the maximum date of delinquency occurred on a particular account, the dollar amount involved and the rating at the time of delinquency
41) Historical status is applied directly by the credit grantor and displays in four columns: the first column for the account and the second, third and fourth columns for the number of months the credit grantor is reviewing the account, over 30 day account, over 60 day account, and over 90 day account, respectively
42) Remarks and dispute codes column is used if the account is in some type of dispute or requires an explanation of the credit condition of the account
43) This position shows the inquiry section of the account. The first number listed indicates the total number of inquiries posted. The final inquiry will be your Trans Union Credit Information Co. subscriber inquiry code along with your subscriber short name. The date you accessed your report and the ECOA designator will also be shown. The loan type and the loan amount (if applicable) is given after the short name
44) Inquiries made over six months prior to your accessing the report will not display for your viewing
45) Collection accounts will be posted, if applicable. The subscriber code for the agency will be listed with the amount of the collection, the ECOA designator, the status of the account, the date reported to the bureau, the date it was paid (if applicable) and the creditor involved
46) Public record information will also be listed on the credit file (if applicable). Public record information will be maintained on a consumer's file in compliance with the Fair Credit Reporting Act. Included in the public record information you will also find the location of the court where the public record was recorded, the court type, the date the public record was reported to the bureau, the ECOA designator, any liabilities or assets and the type of public record. Also listed will be the date paid (if applicable), the docket number and the plaintiff and attorney involved in the case
47) Miscellaneous information that may appear here
48) A consumer statement may appear here
49) Indicates the end of the last page of the credit report

"END OF CREDIT REPORT"

MISC SEE FILE ON MARY ANDERSON
CONSUMER STATEMENT: DINERS CLUB BILL DOES NOT CORRESPOND WITH RESTAURANT RECEIPT

Trans Union Credit Information Co.

| CONTROL NUMBER | OPER. NO. | BATCH NO. | DEPT. NUMBER | REPORT TYPE | ☐ IN FILE | ☐ SINGLE REFERENCE | ☐ TRADE REPORT |
|---|---|---|---|---|---|---|---|
| 95991 | 203 | 543 | 21 | 104 | ☐ EMPLOY & TRADE REPORT | ☐ FULL REPORT | ☐ PREV.M.T REPORT |

**Trans Union Credit Information Co.**
New York/New Jersey Division
95 - 25 Queens Boulevard
Rego Park, New York 11374

| | DATE RECEIVED | DATE MAILED | WATCH CRITERIA |
|---|---|---|---|
| | 06/14/83 | | |
| | DATE TRADE CLEARED | DATE EMPLOY VERIFIED | INCOME VERIFIED |

## CONFIDENTIAL REPORT

FOR (I) ZNY5200

IN FILE SINCE 11/76

| REPORT ON (NAME) | SOCIAL SECURITY NUMBER | SPOUSE'S NAME |
|---|---|---|
| VAIRO, DOUGLAS ANTHONY | | |

| CURRENT ADDRESS | MKT AREA | SPOUSE SOCIAL SECURITY NO. |
|---|---|---|
| NEW AS OF 6/83 , LONG BEACH NY. 11561 | #17 NY | |

| PRESENT EMPLOYER AND ADDRESS | CLOCK # | POSITION | DATE VERIFIED | SINCE | INCOME BASIS |
|---|---|---|---|---|---|
| TROPICANA | | DRIVER | 5/83R | | |

| BIRTH DATE 56-E | NUMBER OF DEPENDENTS INCLUDING SPOUSE → | OWNS/RENTS/BOARDS | TEL. NO. 432-0503 |
|---|---|---|---|

| FORMER ADDRESSES | FROM | TO |
|---|---|---|
| E ROCKAWAY NY. 11518 | 11/82R | 6/83R |
| , LONG BEACH NY. 11561 | | 11/82R |

| FORMER EMPLOYER AND ADDRESS | CLOCK # | POSITION | DATE VERIFIED | SINCE | INCOME BASIS |
|---|---|---|---|---|---|
| SELF EMP WHITESTONE NY. | | | 11/76R | | |

| SPOUSE'S EMPLOYER AND ADDRESS | CLOCK# | POSITION | DATE VERIFIED | SINCE | INCOME BASIS |
|---|---|---|---|---|---|

| SUBSCRIBER NAME / ACCOUNT NUMBER | SUBSCRIBER CODE / COLLATERAL | DATE OPENED | ECOA / TYPE LOAN | HIGH CREDIT / CREDIT LIMIT | DATE CLOSED/VERIFIED / TERMS | BALANCE OWING / DATE | AMOUNT PAST DUE / AMOUNT | NPPD / MOP | PAYMENT PATTERN / NO OF MONTHS 30-60 60-90 90+ | TYPE ACCOUNT & MOP / REMARKS |
|---|---|---|---|---|---|---|---|---|---|---|
| CHEMICAL BK PC B1253 206 | | 4/82 | I | $500 | 4/82P | $0 | $0 | | 1 | C01 |
| CHEMICAL BK MC B9965 206 | | 12/81 | I | $1908 $2000 | 4/83A | $1767 | $0 | | 1111X1111111 | R01 |
| CHEMICAL VISA B1277 1206 | | 1/82 | I | $1862 $2000 | 4/83A | $1721 | $0 | | 111111111111 | R01 |
| CHEMICAL BK IL B1115 93000 | US | 11/81 | I | $2715 | 4/83A 36M75 | $1433 | $0 | | 11111X11X1X1 | I01 |
| MFG HANOVER IL B3137 863C | TITLE N Y PAU | 2/78 | I | $1594 | 7/80C 36M44 | $0 | $0 | | X11111111111 | IUR |
| GMAC 7019 | F5100070 AU | 5/77 | M | $3189 | 5/80C 36M88 | $0 | $0 | 0 | 111111111111 36 0 0 0 | IUR |

| INQR 5 | DATE | ECOA | SUBCODE | SUBNAME | TYPE | AMT |
|---|---|---|---|---|---|---|
| | 6/14/83 | I | ZNY5200 | TUCIC CUST REL | | |
| | 5/23/83 | I | BNY1510 | EAST NY SAV | PL | 4000 |

SEE REVERSE SIDE

BNY820-2/2/82I,GNY8391-4/2/82I,BNY820-4/28/82I
(Chemical)

PAGE 1

FORM CRT/2000 N 1MM 2.83      **CRONUS**      CREDIT REPORTING ON-LINE NETWORK UTILITY SYSTEM

| ☐ IN FILE | ☐ SINGLE REFERENCE | ☐ TRADE REPORT |
|---|---|---|
| ☐ EMPLOY & TRADE REPORT | ☐ FULL REPORT | ☐ PREV A&T REPORT |

## Trans Union Credit Information Co.
New York/New Jersey Division
95 - 25 Queens Boulevard
Rego Park, New York 11374

| DATE RECEIVED | DATE MAILED | WATCH CRITERIA |
|---|---|---|
| DATE TRADE CLEARED | DATE EMPLOY VERIFIED | INCOME VERIFIED |

**CONFIDENTIAL REPORT**  FOR  (I) ZNY5200

| IN FILE SINCE |
|---|

| REPORT ON (NAME) | SOCIAL SECURITY NUMBER | SPOUSE'S NAME |
|---|---|---|
| VAIRO, DOUGLAS ANTHONY | | |

| CURRENT ADDRESS | NEW AS OF 6/83 | MKT AREA | SPOUSE SOCIAL SECURITY NO. |
|---|---|---|---|
| | LONG BEACH NY. 11561 | ✿ | |

| PRESENT EMPLOYER ADDRESS | CLOCK # | POSITION | DATE VERIFIED | SINCE | INCOME BASIS |
|---|---|---|---|---|---|
| | | | | | |

| BIRTH DATE | NUMBER OF DEPENDENTS INCLUDING SPOUSE ⟶ | OWNS/RENTS/BOARDS | TEL. NO. |
|---|---|---|---|

| FORMER ADDRESSES | FROM | TO |
|---|---|---|

| FORMER EMPLOYER AND ADDRESS | CLOCK # | POSITION | DATE VERIFIED | SINCE | INCOME BASIS |
|---|---|---|---|---|---|

| SPOUSE'S EMPLOYER AND ADDRESS | CLOCK# | POSITION | DATE VERIFIED | SINCE | INCOME BASIS |
|---|---|---|---|---|---|

| SUBSCRIBER NAME | SUBSCRIBER CODE | DATE OPENED | ECOA | HIGH CREDIT | DATE CLOSED/ VERIFIED | BALANCE OWING | AMOUNT PAST DUE | NPPD | PAYMENT PATTERN | | | TYPE ACCOUNT & MOP |
|---|---|---|---|---|---|---|---|---|---|---|---|---|
| ACCOUNT NUMBER | | COLLATERAL | TYPE LOAN | CREDIT LIMIT | TERMS | DATE | AMOUNT | MOP | NO OF MONTHS | 30-59 | 60-89 | 90+ | REMARK |

PRMO  2 D36d-1/83,068-3/83

✿✿END OF CREDIT REPORT✿✿

SEE REVERSE SIDE

84

Credit Reporting Procedures

Credit reporting agencies must work under federal guidelines. At the same time, they must be responsible for the information that is processed for both the institutions and the banks seeking information. Also, credit bureaus don't want to have problems with misinformation.

Unfortunately, these credit bureaus do not have any control over what is being reported. They only collect and store information. They do not rate your report, and they do not alter your report without written confirmation either from you, the consumer, or from a reporting agency such as a bank or lending institution. If you want to change a discrepancy that is minor, such as address, they will correct that for you without much problem.

However, if you are looking to change something that is significant, such as the date an account was opened or closed, what the credit limit is or the terms, they have to verify that information with the source of the disputed information. Even if you can show them by your records that the information reported is incorrect, they will go back to the financial institution and verify the information. If they don't, they may be subject to federal penalties.

Several years ago, a couple advertised that they would straighten out your credit for a small fee. They were working for the credit reporting agencies, and they would change your report without checking with the lenders. This is highly illegal. Even when employees of the credit reporting agency want to pull up their own reports, they must have a supervisor with them to verify what they're doing. Otherwise, it would be easy for someone to get a job at a credit reporting agency, pull up his own credit file, and change it. The agencies are careful about the way information is exchanged, and protective of the information on your report. If it seems as though you're not getting anywhere with an agency, it's not the individual who is trying to give you a hard time. These employees are only doing their jobs, the same as you do your job. Remember to be polite – and persistent.

You need to be courteous, because the people you are dealing with have the power to do a lot of things: They can speed things up, slow them down or, if you are particularly abusive, not help you at all.

Credit reporting agencies go by certain rules, but they have some latitude.

If you are polite, they will often go out of their way to do things for you. They might do things that are marginally in your favor, rather than going through the whole process of verifying, if they feel that you are honest.

Another thing about credit reporting procedures is that no one is allowed to check your credit unless you sign a statement giving them authorization. Usually, when you sign those statements, at the bottom of your application it says that they will be allowed to check your credit any time they feel it is necessary and they will be able to exchange information with other creditors as they see fit. Some companies may not disclose such information, which can be a problem for you: If you have an excellent track record with them, it may not show up on your report, but if you have a poor track record, they will put that on your report. In such cases, a letter to the creditor will often persuade it to release the information to a new credit grantor.

Limited and Automatic Subscribers

Limited subscribers do not report on a monthly basis – not because the government or the credit reporting agency limits their reporting, but because that's how they choose to do business. That is frequently a financial decision, because the more you use a credit bureau the more you pay in service fees. That's how the credit bureaus make their money. They collect fees from their sub- scribers and most of their subscribers are lending institutions.

A limited subscriber chooses to report your credit only several times during the lifetime of your loan. An example would be major oil cards or American Express, Diners Club, and many of the other travel and entertainment cards. The only time they check your credit is when you initially apply for a line of credit. They will see what history you have, and if they decide to grant you credit, that's the last time they'll report until you become delinquent or have a problem. Then they will report that delinquency to the credit bureau. It may seem unfair that they report only bad information, but life isn't always fair.

If you have accounts with limited subscribers, keep a ledger of your payments and balances. That way, if you apply for loans, you can submit a photocopy of your ledger, showing the lines of credit and your good payment history, and ask the lender to contact your creditor for confirmation.

Automatic subscribers report on a monthly basis, though they may not report every month. They'll show your account as being current or past due. They're the best type of accounts, because they show how many months you have had your account open.

Don't be too upset about some of these limited subscribers not reporting the amount that's due. They probably carry low balances, making monthly reporting too expensive. However, some types of limited subscribers have large balances like second mortgages. If your second mortgage is not reported and you need the credit history you can use your cancelled checks or get a VOM from your mortgage company.

Who Can Check Your Credit Report?

This is something we went over earlier. Many institutions are allowed to check your credit. You may not even be aware of them.

Employers are allowed to check your credit for certain positions. If you want to become a contractor, or if you want to become a broker in real estate, some local governments run a credit report. Strange? They do that because they want to make sure that you are solvent and responsible. They don't want somebody coming into their county, running up a lot of bills, and then running away.

In this situation, the government is taking some responsibility for whom they allow to have a license in their area. Unscrupulous people have been known to move from place to place to ply their craft. They rip off a lot of people and move on.

Unfortunately, such checks won't protect everyone. In the mid 80's, a gentleman by the name of Bernard Santinero in Port Charlotte, Florida, opened a real estate/title company, along with several other businesses. He stayed in business for several years. He had raised some capital and he showed good credit reports. He did everything to show that he was doing well. He got as much money from investors as he possibly could and then he took off. He ended up leaving the country with more than $5 million of investors' money.

People who are not allowed to check your credit report include your neighbors or a business to which you're not applying for credit but with which you plan to trade. In general, you must consent in writing to have your credit checked.

If you find that someone has checked your credit, do not hesitate to write and ask why.

Federal Trade Commission Complaints about Credit Bureaus

If you feel that a credit bureau has violated any of your rights, you have the right to file a complaint with the FTC.

If you are not sure where to write, you can write to the main office in Washington, D.C. The addresses and telephone numbers are as follows:

Headquarters:

Federal Trade Commission

Pennsylvania Avenue and Sixth Street, N.W.

Washington, DC 20580

(202) 523-3830

Regional Offices:

|  |  |
| --- | --- |
| 1718 Peachtree Street, NW, Atlanta, GA 30367 | 404-881-4836 |
| 150 Causeway Street, Boston, MA 02114 | 617-223-6621 |
| 55 East Monroe Street, Chicago, IL 60603 | 312-353-4423 |
| 118 St. Clair Avenue, Cleveland, OH 44114 | 216-522-4207 |
| 8303 Elmbrook Drive, Dallas, TX 75247 | 214-767-7050 |
| 1405 Curtis Street, Denver, CO 80201 | 303-837-2271 |
| 11000 Wilshire Boulevard, Los Angeles, CA 90024 | 213-209-7575 |
| 26 Federal Plaza, New York, NY 10278 | 212-264-1207 |
| 450 Golden Gate Avenue, San Francisco, CA 94102 | 415-556-1270 |
| 915 Second Avenue, Seattle, WA 98174 | 206-442-4655 |

# CHAPTER 5

## CREDIT IMPROVEMENT

Four Credit Improvement Techniques

There are four ways to improve your credit.

1. Check your reports and get them corrected. This is probably the easiest and can improve your credit rating dramatically. Get a copy of your credit report from all the major bureaus to which you are reported. Compare these reports. You will find that the information they contain differs. Some reports will contain paid-off loans that don't appear on other reports. By sending copies of the reports that show paid-off loans to the bureaus that don't show this information, you can have it put on all of your reports. Most credit reporting agencies readily add this favorable information to your report since it comes from another agency.

2. Ask your creditors to report accounts that are paid in full. Your creditors will most likely have to do this manually. Ask anyone sending a letter or information about you to a third party to send a copy of the letter to you, so that you know exactly what is being reported about you, and keep a copy for your file. Send this favorable information to the credit bureaus and request that it be made a part of your report.

3. Remove negative items, or "dings." We'll discuss this in the next section.

4. Add a consumer statement to your report. If you are writing about more than one item, write about each separately. Keep these statements brief and to the point. The credit reporting agency can help you write your consumer statement if you like. However, make sure that it is done to your complete satisfaction before you agree to having it entered on your report. These statements remain on your report for approximately six years.

Removing Dings and Some Unfavorable Information

You can remove dings in several ways. One is to write to the credit agency and dispute the derogatory information. The credit reporting agency will then investigate your claim with the creditors. If the creditor does not respond within a reasonable time, then the derogatory item must be removed from your record.

Be advised that the negative information can be reinstated on your credit report if and when the company does reply to the credit bureau. Simply stated, if the credit bureau does not receive a response from the creditor within a reasonable period of time (45 days) they must, by law, remove the disputed information. However, if the creditor responds 90 days later then the disputed information is "reinstated" on your credit report.

If you are disputing information about a company that is now "out of business" the disputed information will be permanently deleted from your report because the credit bureau cannot verify the information and therefore must be removed.

Another way to remove dings is to contact the creditor directly and negotiate. This may not always work, but it is worth trying.

Whenever you deal with credit agencies, always be calm and non-threatening. Never, under any circumstances, use foul or abusive language! Always send your letters via certified mail and keep a photocopy of each letter in your file.


Preventing Credit Problems

Being careful with credit cards and your bills can save you a great deal of grief. In general:

Never sign a blank receipt.

Always destroy all the carbons.

Notify the credit card companies every time you change your address.

Always reconcile your credit card accounts.

Keep your credit cards in a safe place.

Keep all information about credit cards  in a safe place.     Include your card
        numbers, the phone numbers and addresses of the companies that issued

them, their expiration dates, your credit limits, and all pertinent information in case they become lost or stolen. This will enable you to notify the companies immediately.

Save all your receipts. Take a business-size envelope, put the bank's name on top of it, the year you are using that card, and the name of the card, whether it's a Mastercard, Visa, etc. Keep these envelopes in a file. Every time you make a purchase with that particular card or get a billing statement, put it in that particular envelope. That makes it easy at the end of the year. You've got all the information on each individual card in one envelope and you can figure out whatever you need to by using that system.

Never, never, never, lend your card to anyone unless it's a close family member. Even then, be very careful.

Avoid giving your credit card number over the phone if the call is incoming. If you made the call, presumably you know whom you called.

Sign your card as soon as you receive it.

You may want to join one of the companies that keep all your credit cards on file. You get stickers that go on your credit cards notifying anyone who has found or stolen your card that you have notified the company, so all your cards are canceled. That way, if you have 10 or 15 cards, you can simply call the 800 number, and they'll cancel all the cards that you report as lost or stolen. They'll also have new cards reissued in your name. That saves you calls to 10 or 15 places. Many credit-card issuers offer such services, as do some automotive clubs. In addition, here is a list of the companies that do this: (we are not necessarily endorsing these companies. For your convenience we are providing you with two of the many companies that are available in this field)

Credit Care Service Bureau
640 N. LaSalle, Suite 440
Chicago, IL 60610-3731
Telephone: 312-649-0720 Toll-free: 800-336-0220

Safecard Services, Inc.
3001 East Pershing Blvd.
Cheyenne, WY 82001
Telephone: 307-771-2700 Toll-free: 800-290-8625

Be just as careful with paying your bills. Three problems arise frequently:

Change of address. You must make sure that as soon as you get your new address, you contact your creditors in writing and by telephone. Do both just to make sure. This is your responsibility – not your creditors' responsibility. You can't expect your creditors to send you a bill if they don't know where to find you.

Late or skipped payments. Many people go on vacation and forget to send or arrange to send payments that should be made before their return. Don't make this mistake. If you plan to be away longer than three weeks, have a trust- ed person send your payments for you. Being on vacation is no excuse for not paying on time. It only shows that you are not responsible.

Payments lost in the mail. This problem is out of your control. Our mail delivery system is fairly accurate, though slow. We have talked to several lend- ing institutions about when you are considered 30 days late and have found that you are not reported as being 30 days late until you have missed two consecutive payments. Some lenders give you the benefit of the doubt when it comes to reporting you 30 days late if you miss one payment because they realize that mail can get lost and that people do go on vacation and forget to send payments early or have them sent by someone else. Creditors will always send a friendly reminder on the next bill. By paying the amount in arrears, your account may not be adversely affected on your credit report, but you rest assured that your creditor keeps track of "your late payments".

How to Control Your Credit

Here's a rule of thumb: Don't incur personal debt equal to more than 20 percent of your income. This does not include mortgage payments or household payments.

Never make purchases of less than $25 with your credit cards. These purchases add up quickly and you probably wouldn't make many of them if a credit card were not available.  If you are in complete control, and never get in over your head, have a card that gives miles for dollars, then you are the exception. You might make all your purchases on the card to accumulate miles, but only if you always pay on time: no finance charges and no compulsive spending. Unfortunately, credit spending can be like an addiction. You must stay in control of your credit because, used improperly, it can inflict severe emotional strain. Once you get in a hole, it's very difficult to get out. It can consume you to the point where you wake up in the morning and go to bed at night thinking about your problem. It robs you of your sense of humor. Don't let that happen to you. Don't let credit control you. You control your credit.

Monthly Delinquencies

When a financial institution gives credit, it expects to receive payment promptly. However, this doesn't always happen, and the lending institution must set about collecting its money in as efficient a manner as possible.

Usually, this process starts with in-house collection procedures.  When the delinquency becomes more severe, the loan is turned over to a collection agency. If you get into this situation, collection agencies will classify you as a deadbeat. They will declare open season on you, because you will have shown that you are not willing to work anything out to pay off the loan. The collectors will do everything they can legally do to collect that money from you. The financial institution is no longer interested in keeping you as a customer. This is one of the reasons why we recommend that you deal with your creditors directly to see what you can work out before you are classified as a deadbeat.

The following is a month-by-month description of what happens to a delinquency:

One Month Delinquent:

Any account for which no payment has been received during the past billing cycle (usually a 30-day period) is considered slightly delinquent and not yet a serious problem. Payments often cross in the mail, or do not reach their destination in time, due to the fact that many people send in their payments on the due date, not realizing that it takes five to seven days before it is credited to their accounts. The lending institution will usually send a friendly reminder stating the amount that is overdue, with- out relaying a sense of urgency. It usually says, "Perhaps you've forgotten your payment, or if it has crossed in the mail, please accept this as a thank you note."

Most delinquencies are paid when this reminder comes, and most people who fall into this category have not paid because they forgot, lost their statement, or temporarily don't have the money. Actually, there are many reasons why people make late payments, and they are usually for very minor reasons. That is why creditors don't get too upset at the one-month delinquent point, even though you can be up to 59 days late with your payment. Since you are not yet 60 days late your credit report shows 1x30 late.

Two Months Delinquent:

Any account on which payment has not been received during the past two months is considered 60 days or two months delinquent. At this point, the lending institution is more concerned because it doesn't want to lose you as a customer by sending tough and dunning letters. But at the same time, it wants to make sure that it gets paid. Lenders in this situation are walking a fine line. They don't want to scare you or embarrass you into not doing business with them. They will send you several letters separate from and in addition to those you will receive in your regular billing cycle. They usually will not call you at this time, but they want to know if there is a problem and why you have not contacted them to let them know what the problem is. However, they are becoming very concerned because you can be up to an incredible 89 days late.

A friend has many such letters because he got tired of the pressure and did not answer any of his creditors. Many of those letters stated that the lending institution was interested in maintaining him as a customer, and that if there were any problems, he should contact the institution to work out a repayment schedule. Lenders just want to hear from you. If they don't, they assume you are running away and don't want to pay. It is very difficult and embarrassing to tell someone that you don't have money, or that you have lost your job or your business. We know. We've been through it. But if you don't do these things, you will hurt yourself even worse by doing nothing at all.

Three Months Delinquent:

"Three months delinquent" accounts are those that have not made any payments on their last three statements. By this time, lenders realize there is a very serious problem. Obviously, the longer that any debt is over- due, the harder it becomes to collect. If your payments are three months delinquent, you will receive a series of letters stating the seriousness of the problem and pointing out how severely your credit can be damaged. Lenders try very hard to collect and bring you current in order to straighten everything out. But they are usually ready to turn the loan over to a collection agency should the debt become more than 90 days overdue. If you're in this position, get in touch with your creditors and see if they'll accept a $5, $10, or $15 payment at this time every month for the next six months to a year, rather than turn it over to a collection agency. Tell them that you can pay back a certain amount every month. Make it a small, manageable amount until you can get back on your feet. Let them know you are aware that if they turn it over to a collection agency they are going to be giving up somewhere on the order of 40 percent of whatever amount is collected. A collection agency will often discount the amount that is owed just to get you to make a fast payment. For example, if you owe $150, the collection agency will say, "We are ready to resolve this matter, if you will send us a check for $100 now." The collection agency isn't losing anything because it wasn't their money to begin with. You send the collection agency $100; it makes between $50 and $80 on that one letter, and you still have a black mark on your credit record for not paying the full amount.

By the time your payment goes beyond the three months delinquent stage, if you do not offer to try to work something out, the institution will usually decline any further credit that you have available and you will be advised that your account is being handed over to a collection agency or an attorney. For example, if you have a $5,000 credit line with $500 outstanding and you go more than 90 days past due, the lenders will cut off your $5,000 credit and cancel your account. Remember, while you don't generally have any major problems until your account is 90 days delinquent, when you go beyond that, you start getting into some very serious problems. If you're less than a couple of months past due, you can usually work something out with the financial institution.

More Than 120 Days Delinquent:

This is an account on which no payments have been received during the past 120 days or four billing cycles. By this time the account is given to a collection agency. The lending institution no longer has any intention of maintaining you as a customer and will use whatever legal methods it can to collect. If the amount is large, it is usually given to a lawyer. If the amount is small and more readily collectible, it is given to a collection agency first.

If the collection agency is unsuccessful and the amount owed is large enough, it is given to a lawyer for litigation. Sometimes the collection agency will turn it back over to the company and the company will just write it off. That all depends on the lenders' policies and how they feel at the time. Obviously, if a financial institution has a money crunch and doesn't have enough bad loan reserves put aside to cover these losses, it is going to be very aggressive in collecting everything it can. Put yourself in the lenders' shoes. Suppose you had loaned $100 each to 10 of your friends. That's a total of $1,000. If things are going along real well for you and they are paying you back a couple of dollars a month each and then they stop paying you, you're not going to worry about the fact that you are not collecting a couple dollars a month. On the other hand, if all of a sudden you were to come into a financial crunch and you needed money badly, you would be on the phone with them every single day, or seeing them in person, or writing them letters asking them to cough up whatever they can. It works the same in any type of business. The hungrier you are, the more aggressive you are in getting what you need.

Try to work it out with your lending institution first, even if it has gone to a collection agency or a lawyer. See if you can negotiate with the lending institution to calm things down so they don't get too far out of hand. Many of the lending institutions from which you borrow money have a clause in their disclosures stating that you as the borrower are responsible for all reasonable legal and attorney's fees and any fees associated with that lending institution having to collect a bad debt from you; so before these costs get too high or insurmountable, negotiate with your lenders. They do not want your blood. They want to get as much of their money back as possible, and they will work with you if you can offer them any hope of achieving that goal.

## Declines

Your credit application could be rejected for any number of reasons. This is only a brief overview of some of the many reasons for denial. We have included reproductions of actual denial letters from financial institutions in the sample section of Chapter 6. As you will see when you read them, some of the rea- sons for denying credit are less severe than others, and sometimes several reasons for decline will be checked off if they are warranted.

## Excessive Inquiries

Almost every time you apply for credit, the lender will pull a credit report on you. It is then reported on subsequent reports that an inquiry was made on that date by that lender. Therefore, if you were turned down for credit, your next creditor is more likely to turn you down too, although each lending institution has its own policies. Even though you are turned down by two or three companies in a row, that fourth, fifth, and sixth company will sometimes extend credit. Excessive inquiries within a six-month period definitely hurt your chances of obtaining new credit. If you have several inquiries with denials within the past six months, that will often cause a future application to be declined. But here again, some of the inquiries that are on your report can be removed if you did not sign anything allowing that lender to check your credit. Also, look for inquiries that are more than two years old and have those removed, since most inquiries shouldn't be on your report longer than two years. If it says PRM, that means it's a promotional inquiry, and if it's more than six months old that also should be removed from your credit report. Currently, creditors will not see promotional inquiries made by other "potential" creditors.

No Credit History

Another common reason for denial is the lack of a credit history. People who have never applied for credit in their own names or paid back any installment-type loan have no credit history. Sometimes people do not have a credit history because a loan they have been paying is not in their own name. If someone else has co-signed for that loan, perhaps the lending institution is reporting to the credit bureau that the co-signer is the one who is actually making the payments. If this is true in your situation, you need to rectify that situation by having the lending institution forward a copy of its files to the credit bureau stating that you were the actual borrower and the other person was the co-signer. When a credit report is run on an individual and there is no payment pattern or history, the credit report will usually come back showing that no records were found. This can sometimes be worse than having bad credit, because a credit grantor will not be able to tell what type of payment pattern you had in the past. This is a Catch-22 situation. The lending institution is looking for some type of history before it will lend you money. Since you don't have a history, they don't want to lend you money. So, if they won't lend you money to establish a payment pattern, how do you establish a payment pattern to show the banks that you are credit-worthy? Refer to the section on secured credit cards. You can fix the problem of not having any credit history by gradually applying for "easy" credit sources. You build slowly.

## Self-Employment

Many lenders feel that someone who is self-employed presents a greater risk than people who are employed by others. In order for self-employed people to qualify for loans, they usually need to be self-employed in the same business for two years or more. Lenders have different guidelines, so make sure you find out what they are. Lenders will ask self-employed people to submit their last two years' income tax returns. This is a highly personal matter and is entirely up to you as to whether you wish to have a financial institution review your income tax records. If you refuse to give the income tax information, the likelihood is that your credit application will be declined.

## Public Notices

Public notices are items that have been recorded with the county. Examples are bankruptcies, notices of default, foreclosures, judgments, etc.

## Overextended Credit

When creditors look at your application, they take into consideration your monthly income and your expenses. If you are already overextended, they will deny your application. It's obvious why they would deny you credit under those circumstances. One exception would be a mortgage that consolidates most or all of your debt into a much lower payment.

## Negative and Derogatory Credit

When a creditor pulls a credit report on you, he will look to see what your payment history has been. This will tell him whether you: have paid as agreed;

have been 30, 60, or 90 days late; have had any collection agencies try to collect; or have had any judgments, liens, or bankruptcies in the past seven to 10 years. The more negative or derogatory marks on your credit report, the more severe the lending institution will be in its lending policy towards you. However, if you are able to satisfactorily explain why some of these dings or derogatory remarks are on your report, they might be overlooked.

Should you be denied credit, find out the reasons and try to rectify the problems. When you receive a decline notice, don't get upset. This is part of doing business. When you're applying for credit, you're working with the law of averages the same as a salesman or any other person selling a product. Your product is your financial situation, and you're trying to obtain the amount of credit that you would feel comfortable with to conduct your business or personal life.

Many salesmen realize that rejection is a part of everyday life. They will make 10 calls for the day and realize that maybe only four people will see them and only one or two people will purchase. If you send out 10 credit card applications, you may get back six declines, two or three requests for additional information, and one that approves you. At that point, you can just leave it the way it is, or you can take those declines and try to turn them into approvals.

If you feel that the reason for the decline is too severe for you to correct, you can still take that decline notice, send it to your credit agency, and get a free report. Sometimes, just by calling on the phone and being pleasant, you are able to get the information over the phone, rather than have them send out a credit report, thus getting the information immediately and saving an inquiry on your report. Whenever you speak with people from the credit reporting agency, always be kind and courteous. By giving you the information over the telephone, they are doing you a great service. Make sure you let them know that you appreciate their help.

Giving you information over the phone is the exception rather than the rule, however. Most credit reporting agencies require that you send in a written request for your credit report. Don't feel bad when they require this. They are only doing their job, which is to protect the information that is in their files.

Suppose you were to obtain someone else's name, Social Security number, address, and whatever other information the credit bureau required, and you were to call to find out what was in that person's file. That would be fraud. The cred- it bureau people are only trying to do their job.

Do not accept all denials as final. Discover the specific reason for decline and see if you can rectify the problem.

Fix Your Credit With the Wage Earner Plan

By using a little-known method called "The Wage Earner Plan," you can keep your credit partially intact while reducing your payment to your creditors. The Wage Earner Plan is part of Chapter 13 of the federal Bankruptcy Code.

This is a court-supervised debt consolidation plan. All your debts are turned over to a federal court for a payment from a portion of your income. You must earn your living from salary, wages, or commissions. This plan is not for self-employed people. That is why the name is Wage Earner Plan. This is not absolute bankruptcy, since none of your debts are actually discharged.

You must design your own payment plan. Your payments must be enough to pay off all your creditors within 36 months. This can be extended for an additional 24 months. Those are the two conditions that must be met before the court will approve your plan. When the federal court accepts your plan, all your creditors must accept the plan because it has been approved by the court. You will not be able to borrow any money during this time.

Follow the steps below to set the Wage Earner Plan in motion:
Step 1:
Go to the U.S. District Court in your area and speak to the Trustee.

Step 2:
Fill out all the forms that the Trustee gives you. You will be listing all your income and debts. Remember to fill them out completely and honestly. If a question does not apply or the information is not available, write "N/A." This will avoid delays because people will realize that you have filled out your

application in full and they have not received an incomplete application.

Step 3:

Pay a filing fee. This fee will vary from county to county, so call the Clerk in your area.

As soon as you complete these steps, the court will issue a restraining order to all the creditors you have listed. Be sure to list all your creditors! If you forget to list someone, it will cause problems.

The restraining order does the following things:

1. Stops all interest and late payment fees.
2. Stops your creditors from attaching or garnishing any of your wages.
3. Stops your creditors from seizing any of your property.
4. Stops all legal action (only from the creditors you listed) against you.
5. Stops creditors from contacting, harassing, or threatening you.

It usually takes about 90 days before your court date arrives. When this day rolls around, you will be required to pay another fee of approximately $25. Several more benefits of the plan are:

1. Payments are made to fit your income, budget, and pay periods. For example, you do not have to make weekly payments if you get paid once a month.

2. It will reduce your payments to an affordable amount.

3. If an unsecured creditor fails to file a claim within 180 days, you don't have to pay that creditor. Well over 50 percent of all creditors fail to file. Should a creditor fail to file, it would be entirely up to you whether or not you repay that creditor at a later date. It would be up to your own standards and morals. After all, you did borrow the money with the promise to repay.

We don't believe in bankruptcy or in using legal techniques to discharge debts that were willingly incurred in many cases. However, if the debt is pressing heavily on your shoulders and you really need to get out from under the heavy strain, then you should consider these methods. Your life is more important than money. If you had an accident and your medical bills were hundreds of thousands of dollars, you might elect to use one of the methods in this book to get yourself back on your feet. Some people who have filed bankruptcy in the past have repaid the creditors once they got back on their feet. We suggest bankruptcy only as a last resort. Use every negotiating technique with your creditors before you resort to bankruptcy. You may be very pleasantly surprised to learn that most of your creditors will work with you. If, however, you are hopelessly in debt, use the bankruptcy laws. They are there to give you a clean start.

Some Disadvantages to the Wage Earner Plan

Since there are several disadvantages to the Wage Earner Plan, it is recommend that you deal with your creditors directly. Some of the disadvantages of the Wage Earner Plan are:

1. It may be listed on your credit report for up to seven years.
2. You need the approval of all of your secured creditors.
3. You cannot take on additional debt while on this program.
4. Lenders tend to look on this program with the same attitude as bankruptcy.

Since everyone's problems are unique, you will need to evaluate each situation carefully. Only then can you decide on which method will best suit your situation.

Bankruptcies, Judgments, and Liens

Bankruptcies

Things to consider before filing:

1. Are any other options available?
2. Some people feel bankruptcy is a disgrace since they realize that they morally and legally owe that money.
3. You may be embarrassed and humiliated by having your entire financial history laid out in front of the court.
4. Will it be better to have a 10-year bankruptcy on your report or just seven years of charge-offs?
5. How bad should things be before you file for bankruptcy? This is entirely your decision. Make sure you find a competent attorney. The paperwork is unbelievable, and you don't want to goof. If your attorney goofs, he is responsible. If you goof, you can't sue yourself. A good attorney can cost in the neighborhood of $500. If your debts are many or complicated, then the fee will be higher.

The following debts are not discharged with bankruptcy:

1. Any debt you forget to list on your petition.

2. Alimony.

3. Child support.

4. Most taxes owed. Usually that includes federal, state, and city taxes.

5. Any debts caused by theft, embezzlement, or any fraudulent method.

6. Any items purchased just prior to filing. This is looked upon as last-minute theft.

7. Guaranteed student loans.

So, is bankruptcy really for you? Debtors will often take the easy way out by filing bankruptcy without thinking of the possible consequences. Sometimes, financial problems can torment a person day and night.

Let's discuss what bankruptcy really does. Straight bankruptcy is probably the debtor's most powerful tool. It's a way to make most debts disappear without having to repay them. It may sound like an easy solution, but it is not, and many debtors would not benefit from it. Although bankruptcy is considered to result in a fresh clean start and freedom from past debts, that is not completely true.

If you decide to file for bankruptcy, follow the steps outlined above. But before you decide to file for bankruptcy, sit down and carefully think through all your options. You may be able to bounce back in better shape than if you take that plunge into the world of bankruptcy.

Since bankruptcy, judgments, and liens are recorded in the courthouse, it is up to the credit bureaus to send their people to the courthouse files to obtain this information. The information is often reported in error by the credit agencies. You can fight this inaccuracy and sometimes have the bankruptcy removed from your report.

When you apply for credit, the application usually asks if you have declared bankruptcy within the past seven to 14 years. Sometimes it will say "ever." If you have declared bankruptcy within that time and don't put it on your credit application, then you are filing a fraudulent document. Sometimes the credit agency overlooks bankruptcies, judgments, and liens by accident.

Reaffirmation

When you decide to declare bankruptcy and the proceedings are finalized, creditors will sometimes try a tactic that most consumers are unaware of to collect their money. They will tell you that they are willing to reopen that loan with you and lend you more money. For example, if you claim bankruptcy and one of your creditors was owed $1,000, a representative of that institution may write to you and explain that he realizes the financial hardship that you have gone through, and he wishes to still help you since you did have a good account with them for many years. He says that they are willing to lend you $1,500 to help you get back on your feet, as a gesture of good faith.

Many people believe the institution is ready to lend them $1,500. But this is not the case. The reality is, they will reopen the loan for $1,500 but the proceeds that you will actually receive will be $500. What the creditor in effect has done is put you back on the books for that original $1,000 that you owed and discharged through bankruptcy. You may be tempted to go ahead and take that money, but you must realize that you now owe a $1,500 debt and you have only $500 in hand. Also, according to the law, you're not allowed to claim bankruptcy for at least another seven years. Since the creditor realizes that you have no protection under the bankruptcy law, you are fair game to collect that money.

Be aware that these are some tactics that can be used. We're not saying that they are common. We are saying that they are tactics that creditors have used in the past. So be careful.


The Lure of Easy Bankruptcy The

following is a true story.

A husband-and-wife team of practicing psychiatrists, with joint income of $78,000, accumulate personal debts totaling $22,000 plus a $33,000 mortgage on their comfortable, suburban New York home. They are not in arrears, or even over their heads. They simply want more discretionary spending power.

The solution? They file for bankruptcy and reduce their debt load to less than 10 cents on the dollar, repayable on an extended painless schedule. Notes an officer of one of their finance companies: "They could have sold the house or refinanced the mortgage and paid off all their bills in full. But why should they?" Clearly, their morals were out to lunch.

Traditionally, personal bankruptcy has been a gut-wrenching last resort for people so deeply in debt and so harried by creditors that no other option seemed viable. The typical profile: low-income, undereducated; very young or over 65. Rootless non-homeowners.

The profile today: people with good jobs, quite often two-income families with household incomes as high as six figures declare bankruptcy not from dire necessity, but merely to rid themselves of debts that cramp their lifestyle. Rationale: society owed them the education. Keep-up-with-Joneses types. From suburban executives to Park Avenue professionals, they are unwilling to live within their means.

Making it easier: passage of the Federal Bankruptcy Act of 1978. This significantly liberalized personal filing procedure in the name of consumer rights. Chapter 7 makes no reference to the debtor's income. It permits debtors to clear the slate by turning over all their assets except those specifically exempted to creditors. Among the exemptions: up to $7,500 equity in the debtor's house ($15,000 if both spouses file); $4,000 in accrued dividends; $1,200 in automobile equity; $500 in jewelry; $200 per category of household items (clothing, books, etc.) and more.

Chapter 13 requires that debtors show only a regular income to handle a reasonable three-year payback plan. Court definition of reasonable: as little as 1 percent to 10 percent of the total debts, even where 50 percent or more could easily be managed. Payoff: either way, the law does not require a bankrupt individual to show financial hardship. The debtor merely claims bankruptcy, eliminates most outstanding debt, and keeps most tangible assets. Even the stigma is gone, because the law forbids use of the term "bankrupt" when legally describing a "debtor."

The economic recession. The Federal Reserve Board's credit controls which were imposed early in 1980 tightened the screws on many people with debts. Federal Trade Commission approval of the right of lawyers to advertise their services. This opened the eyes of debtors to the opportunities. Result:

lawyers are aggressively promoting this new way out of debt. Focus: California, Florida, New York.

Two things lawyers don't mention in their ads: 1) Lawyers always get paid upfront, even before filing the papers; some even accept credit cards. 2) The bankruptcy goes on the client's credit record for up to 10 years, meaning the slate is not clean. Clients cannot even seek to square matters with past creditors. Reason: reaffirmation of debts, once they have been wiped out, is prohibited, unless the offer is court-approved. (Chances for that are slim.)


Collection Agencies

In this and following sections we will discuss some collection agency tactics, why collection agencies are brought into the picture, what their rights are, what your rights are, and how they proceed to collect their debts. We will also discuss what your rights are to dispute debts and what the consequences are if you should not pay a debt that is yours. You will also see some actual collection letters.

We can certainly understand why collection agencies use the tactics that they do. This does not mean that a collection agency should overstep its bounds by being abusive, harassing, or doing anything the law says it is not allowed to do. There is no reason to treat people like pieces of dirt or as though they were less than human because they owe a debt. There is nothing wrong with a creditor trying to collect money owed him from a debtor, but at the same time, he should deal in a fair and reasonable manner.

For example, we received a letter from a collection agency which came through the mail without any postal mark on it. The post office must have over-looked stamping it. When received, the first letter asked for payment by the 20th of that month. The letter was not received until the 19th. Hardly a reasonable period of time in which to pay the bill, and quite possibly the collection agency sent that letter out purposely only a day or two before the payment was due. It was trying to create a sense of urgency, which in the mail order business is a most effective tool. If something gets put aside it's forgotten. Therefore, creative advertising will persuade someone to take action immediately. That is usually what's in many collection letters. They say you must take care of this now before such and such happens. They try to prompt you into an action while you are reading that letter.

On the envelope we received, it was made to look as though it were from an attorney's office. On the envelope it just gave the address. However, on the letter, between the name of the company and the address, it says in big letters: Services limited to collections. The reason is that the Fair Debt Collection Act says that a collection agency is not allowed to advertise on the envelope that it is anything other than a collection agency or that you are a deadbeat or any derogatory information of that nature. However, on the face of its letter, it is allowed to explain exactly what services it offers. The reason it put the "services limited to collections" is so there is no misunderstanding that it may be any- one else, such as attorneys.

How to Handle Collection Agencies

Usually, in negotiations, there are no set rules. Negotiation is whatever the borrower and lender will agree on. However, this is not true when you deal with collection agencies, since the inception of the Fair Debt Collection Act.

This law is for the protection of consumers against unethical bill collectors. We've included a copy of the law in Chapter 7 of this manual. It gives the Federal Trade Commission the power of enforcement. To break down the Fair Debt Collection Act into a simpler form, there are several things that collection agencies are forbidden to do. We will list those here in a more concise form.

1.      They cannot continue to contact the consumer after the consumer has specifically notified them not to do so. At this point, the collection agency may only notify you one more time and the only alternative is to take legal action or forget the whole thing. If the bill is for a small amount, they will usually, but not always, forget the whole thing.

2.      They are not allowed to threaten legal action or anything else of that nature unless they specifically plan to do so. Also, they are not allowed to threaten that they are going to have you arrested.

3.      They are not allowed to ask the consumer for a postdated check unless

they plan to deposit that check on the due date of the check. In the past, many collection agencies would ask the consumer to send in a postdated check for a month later and as soon as they received the check they would deposit it that day. You would think that a bank would not honor these checks because they are postdated, but the banks don't check the dates, and the checks go through. The collection agency needs to notify you 72 hours before it makes the deposit. Any funds the consumer hands over to the collection agency must be applied in a way agreed upon. For example, if it is supposed to go toward interest first, and then the late fees, and then the principal, then that's the only way the collection agency is allowed to post that money. If it goes all toward principal and interest and late fees are to be paid at the end, that is the only way the collection agency is allowed to apply the funds.

4. Collection agencies are not allowed to use fake names. They are not allowed to say that they are a law firm, or a credit bureau, or a government agency or anything of that nature.

5. Collection agencies are not allowed to write to anyone besides you or your attorney. They can try to locate you by asking anyone else where you are, or to find out if you have left town. Even under those circumstances, the collection agency is not allowed to tell these people that they are trying to collect any money from you.

6. Collection agencies are not allowed to use foul language, harass you, or mentally abuse you. They cannot threaten violence or harm to property, reputation, or bodily injury.

7. Collection agencies are not allowed to continually harass someone on the telephone either at home or at work by calling and not saying who they are, by making repeated phone calls, by calling and hanging up or by any- thing else of that nature.

8. Collection agencies are not allowed to call the consumer during incon- venient or off hours. They are allowed to call only between 8 a.m. and 9 p.m. your time. If they are in California and you are in New York, they have to adjust to your time zone. These rules apply only if the consumer

doesn't agree otherwise. However, if the consumer does agree, the collection agency may call during those hours that are agreed upon with the consumer. According to law, they are not supposed to call the consumer more than several times in a week. However, a phone call is very hard to prove and it is more personal than a letter, so many collection agencies will, in fact, call more than several times in a week. Sometimes they will call several times in one day. This is just another means they have to prompt someone into taking action that day. As far as your telephone goes, there are two ways that are quite effective in stopping the collection agency from harassing you. One thing you can do that's pretty drastic, admittedly, is to disconnect your phone totally. We certainly don't recommend doing this if you have other business that you are taking care of, and family and friends who need to call, but that is certainly one method at your disposal. The second method is to simply change your telephone number to an unlisted number. That does not guarantee that the collection agency somehow won't track down your number, but it gives you a lot more breathing space and allows you the opportunity to have the collection agencies contact you only in writing. That way, the collection agencies can tell you specifically what they are going to do only in writing. You may find that the tone of the letters is a lot more reasonable than the phone calls you received in the past. The third method is to put an answering machine in the house – and screen your calls. If a collection agency leaves a message that is foul or abusive or threatening, you have it on tape. Also, if you do decide to answer the telephone and the collection agency begins to give you a hard time, you simply need to say that you wish to tape the conversation. A collection agency will often tell you no and will hang up.

9.  Collection agencies are not allowed to advertise or publish a list of deadbeat names. A deadbeat list includes names, addresses, and amounts of money owed. They are not allowed to send these lists to anyone in your community for any reason that would be derogatory to you.

10. Collection agencies are not allowed to contact you by postcard or a letter

indicating on the outside that you owe money or that you are a deadbeat, or that the agency is actually a collection agency.

11. Collection agencies are not allowed to have the consumer incur any expense for communicating with the collection agency. For example, no collect calls.

12. Collection agencies are not allowed to call you at your place of employment if your employer does not permit it. If you give a home phone number they may not call you at work.

Should the collection agency sue you, you have the right to be sued in your own area. It may not sound like it is a big deal, but just suppose that the collection agency was 2,000 miles away. You would have a very difficult time appearing in court. Therefore, you have the right to have the suit brought against you in the judicial district where you live. This way, if you are sued, you will be able to show up in court (it is absolutely imperative that you show up: if you don't, you're going to lose by default).

Most people lie to collection agencies. Don't be one of them! Tell the truth and work with them.

The Best Way to Handle Problems

Communicate with your creditors, and honestly make an effort to work things out. Frequently these situations can be amicably resolved.

Do not agree to terms that are going to suffocate you. For example, if you owe a large sum of money and a creditor or a collection agency tells you that you need to send them $100 a month, don't agree to that unless you can actually pay that amount. Work with your creditors and the collection agencies, and you will find that you get some good results.

Aside from paying the bill in full in one payment, your best option is to work out some type of payment plan. Negotiate.

Credit Counseling Services and Credit Bureau Complaints

The following number is for the Consumer Credit Counseling Service national line: 1-800-388-2227. When you call this number, you will be given the address and telephone number of the Consumer Credit Counseling Service in your area. If you feel that you need counseling in this area, contact the service nearest you.

Federal Trade Commission and Formal Complaints

If you feel that a credit bureau has violated your rights, you should immediately file a formal written complaint with the Federal Trade Commission. It's a good idea to initiate your protest with a phone call to the FTC.

Filing a Complaint

If you feel that you have been discriminated against, or that your rights have been violated under the Equal Credit Opportunity Act, you can file a complaint with the agencies listed below:

For complaints against national banks, write to:
Comptroller of Currency/Consumer Department
> Washington, D.C. 20219

For complaints against non-member insured banks, write to:
Federal Deposit Insurance Corp. (FDIC)
> Customer Affairs
> Washington, D.C. 20429

For complaints against state-chartered banks, write to:
Director of Community Affairs
> Board of Governors of Federal Reserve System
> Washington, D.C. 20551

or the state agency that controls state charters usually called the State Banking and Insurance Commission. A call to your state capitol will locate the appropriate agency. You can also check government websites.

# CHAPTER 6

## SAMPLE LETTERS

---

To help you in dealing with banks credit bureaus, creditors, etc., we've including a variety of sample letters in this chapter:

Make sure that every letter you send is via "certified mail". Keep a copy of every letter you send and attach the certified proof to each letter.

6.1 Sample Request Letter (Secured Credit Card Request Form)

Name
Address
City, State, Zip

Date

Name of Bank
Street Address
City, State and Zip

Certified mail # xxxx xxxx

Dear Sir:

At your first opportunity, please forward to me any available information and requirements, including an application, for a <u>secured</u>
credit card (Visa, MasterCard).

Please specify your savings account or Certificate of Deposit
requirements.

Thank you for your assistance in this matter.

## THIS IS A SERIOUS MATTER.
## PLEASE ACT ACCORDINGLY!

Very truly yours,

(Your Signature)

## 6.2  Credit Request Report  Form

Name
Address
City, State, Zip


Date


Name of Credit Bureau
Street Address of Credit Bureau
City, State, and Zip


Certified mail # xxxx xxxx

Dear Sir:

At your earliest opportunity, please mail me a copy of my credit report. The information needed is listed below.

Name:_____Spouse:_____
Present Address: _____
Previous Address: _____
Address Past 5 Years: _____


Social Security Number:_____Spouse SSN:_____
Credit Denied Last 30 Days? Yes_____No_____
Credit Denied By: _____
Check for $_____(Each Person) enclosed. Thank you.

# THIS IS A SERIOUS MATTER.
# PLEASE ACT ACCORDINGLY!


Yours truly,

(Your Signature)

6.3 Settlement Letter to Creditors, #1 (Out-of-court settlement)

Client's Name
Client's Address
City, State, Zip
Account #

Mr. (Name of Collection Manager)
Name of Creditor
Address of Creditor
City, State, Zip
Certified mail # xxxx xxxx

Dear Sir:

Because of my recurring employment problem, mainly as a result of my poor health, I find it regrettably out of my reach to pay my debts to your fine company. My present modest income is barely enough for me to survive on, leaving nothing for back payments. Unfortunately. I have nothing of value to sell in order to raise cash and satisfy my obligation to you or a host of other creditors in your same position.

However, I feel obligated to your company and am willing to offer a settlement of 25 cents on the dollar as payment in full. My current balance with you is $1,425. I am able to make my $356.25 payment in full (25% of $1,425) next Friday, after I cash my paycheck.

If these terms are acceptable to you, please sign where indicated and return to me immediately.

# THIS IS A SERIOUS MATTER. PLEASE ACT ACCORDINGLY!

Yours truly,
(Your Signature)

Read, Approved and Accepted by: _____  _____

                                       Collection Manager          Date

                                       Witness                   Date

## 6.3 Settlement Letter to Creditors, #2 (Out-of-court settlement.)

Date
Client's Name
Client's Address
City, State, Zip
Account #

Mr. (Collection Manager)
Name of Creditor
Address of Creditor
City, State and Zip
via certified mail # xxxx xxxx

Dear Sir:

As a result of my recent divorce, regrettably I find myself in a difficult financial situation for the first time in my life, and unable to satisfy my debt with your fine company. Unfortunately, after the divorce, I was left with no savings account or items of value which I could sell in order to raise the necessary funds to satisfy my debt owed to you, as well as to all of my other creditors.

Even though most of the charges incurred in your store are from my former spouse, I find myself compelled to make a settlement with you. I am able to pay you 50 cents on the dollar as payment in full in the following fashion:

Current Balance: $850 Amount Owed: $425 (50% of $850)

Payments: January 1, 19__: $125        February 1, 19_: $100
          March 1, 19__: $100          April 1, 19_: $100

If these terms are acceptable, please sign below and forward to me at once. Even though some of my friends who have been in this same position have filed for bankruptcy, I want to avoid this, if possible, since I feel it is not the morally correct thing to do.

Yours truly,


(Your signature)
Client

Read, Approved and Accepted by: _____  _____
                                Collection Manager        Date



                                _____  _____
                                Witness                   Date

## 6.3 Settlement Letter to Creditors, #3

Via Certified Mail, Return Receipt Requested

Name
Address
City, State, Zip

Date

XYZ Company
Street Address
City, State and Zip

Certified mail # xxxx xxxx

RE: Account Number:_____

Dear Sirs:

I am writing in regard to my account with your store.

I recently was laid off my job and am in the process of looking for new employment. I have fallen behind with my payments and would like to work out a repayment plan with your company. I am able to pay $10.00 per month until I am working again. I am enclosing a check for $10.00 to apply towards my account.

Please accept this payment and my proposal for future payments until I am able to fulfill the original terms of my contract.

Please make this letter a part of my file.

# THIS IS A SERIOUS MATTER.
# PLEASE ACT ACCORDINGLY!

Thank you.
Sincerely,

(Your Signature)
Name

If these terms are acceptable, please sign below and forward to me at once. Even though some of my friends who have been in this same position have filed for bankruptcy, I will avoid this, if possible, since I feel it is not the morally correct thing to do.

Read, Approved and Accepted by: _____ _____
                                           Collection Manager            Date

## 6.4 Credit Card Application Decline Letter, #1

Dear:

Thank you for your recent credit application which has been given serious and careful consideration. We are required by law to furnish you with the following information:

      1. Description of adverse action taken:____**DECLINE VISA APPLICATION**____

      2. The principal reason(s) for adverse action concerning your credit application is/are:

| | | | |
|---|---|---|---|
| _____ | Credit Application incomplete | _____ | Too short a period of residence |
| _____ | Insufficient credit references | _____ | Temporary residence |
| _____ | Unable to verify credit references | _____ | Unable to verify residence |
| _____ | Temporary or irregular employment | _____ | No credit file |
| _____ | Unable to verify employment | _____ | Insufficient credit file |
| _____ | Length of employment | _____ | Delinquent credit obligations |
| _____ | Insufficient income | _____ | Garnishment, attachment, foreclosure, |
| _____ | Excessive obligations | |     repossession or suit |
| _____ | Unable to verify income | _____ | Bankruptcy |
| _____ | Inadequate collateral | | |

_____ We do not grant credit to any applicant on the terms and conditions you request.

__X__ Other, specify:____OPENED MASTER CARD____

DISCLOSURE OF USE OF INFORMATION OBTAINED FROM AN OUTSIDE SOURCE:

__X__ Disclosure inapplicable

_____ Information obtained in a report from a consumer reporting agency

                        Name:

                        Street Address:

                        City, State:

                        Telephone No:

_____ Information obtained from an outside source other than a consumer agency. Under the Fair Credit Reporting Act, you have the right to make a written request within 60 days of receipt of this notice, for disclosure of the nature of the adverse information.

      3. The Federal Equal Credit Opportunity Act prohibits creditors from discriminating against credit applicants on the basis of race, color, religion , national origin, sex, marital status, age(provided that the applicant has the capacity to enter into a binding contract): because all or part of the applicant's income derives from any public assistance program: or because the applicant has in good faith exercised any right under the Consumer Credit Protection Act. The federal agency that administers compliance with this law concerning this creditor is the Comptroller of the Currency, Consumer Affairs Division, Washington D.C. 20219. We regret that we are unable to accommodate your request for credit and we thank you again for considering our bank.

                                          Sincerely yours,

6.4 Credit Card Application Decline Letter, #2

(Name of Credit Card Company)

Reference Number

Dear:

We would like to take this opportunity to thank you for your interest in (Name of Credit Card).

Unfortunately, we cannot approve your application for Card Membership at this time.

Our decision was based on the information you provided in your application and information contained in a consumer report which we obtained from:

(Name and address of Credit Bureau)

If you request a statement of the specific reasons for our decision within 60 days of the date of this letter, we will furnish this information no later than 30 days after our receipt of your request. Please include the date of this letter and the reference number shown above in your request.

Thank you again for your interest.

Sincerely,

(Name)
New Accounts

## 6.4 Credit Card Application Decline Letter, #3

IMPORTANT INFORMATION

The Federal Equal Credit Opportunity Act and comparable provisions of Massachusetts law, and the Utah Uniform Consumer Credit Code, prohibit creditors from discriminating against credit applicants on the basis of race, color, religion, national origin, sex, marital status, age(provided that the applicant has the capacity to enter into a binding contract); or because all or part of the applicant's income derives from any public assistance program. The Federal Equal Credit Opportunity Act and the Utah Statute also prohibit creditors from discriminating against credit applicants because the applicant has in good faith exercised any right under the Consumer Credit Protection Act. The Federal agency that administers compliance with the Federal law concerning this creditor is the Comptroller of the Currency, Consumer Affairs Division, Washington, D.C. 20219.

ADDITIONAL INFORMATION FOR RESIDENTS OF MAINE, MASSACHUSETTS, NEW YORK, OHIO, UTAH, AND WASHINGTON:

Maine and New York Residents:
If a consumer reporting agency is identified in this letter, you have the right to inspect and receive a copy of the agency's report by contacting the consumer reporting agency.

Massachusetts Residents:
The state agency that administers compliance with the state law is the Massachusetts Commission Against Discrimination, One Ashburton Place, Boston, Massachusetts 02108.

Ohio Residents:
The Ohio laws against discrimination require that all creditors make credit equally available to all credit worthy customers and that credit reporting agencies maintain separate credit histories on each individual upon request. The Ohio Civil Rights Commission administers compliance with this law.

Utah Residents:
The state agency that administers compliance with the state law is the Department of Financial Institutions, Hebert M. Wells Building, 160 East 300 South, 3rd Floor, Salt Lake City, Utah 84111.

Washington Residents:
The Washington State law against discrimination prohibits discrimination in credit transactions because of race, creed, color, national origin, sex, or marital status. The Washington State Human Rights Commission administers compliance with this law.

## 6.5 Sample Consumer Statement, #1

Date:_____


Any CreditBureau
Street Address
Any town, USA
via certified mail # xxxx xxxx

RE: (Name of merchant, Subscriber No._____, Acct. No.__) Dear

Sirs:

I would like the following consumer statement added to my credit report as soon as possible, as it is very pertinent to the unjust and injurious manner in which the referenced account is being reported. Please send me a copy of the updated report after completion of the entry.

This statement is regarding a dispute over defective merchandise which I received from (name of merchant and address) just prior to its closing down. I made several written communications to them, but received no reply. Several calls were unreturned, and when I finally got in contact with the Manager, his attitude was that it was my tough luck. I refused to pay further on the account until I received satisfaction. They never contacted me. I found out about this charge off upon applying for credit with Finance One.

Sincerely,

(Signature)

John Consumer
SSN: _____

## 6.5 Sample Consumer Statement, #2

Date


Any Credit Bureau
Street Address
City, State and Zip
via certified mail # xxxx xxxx


RE: ABC Company, Subscriber No._____, Acct. No. _____

Dear Sir:

I would like the following consumer statement added to my credit report as soon as possible as it is very pertinent to the unjust and injurious manner in which the referenced account is being reported. Please send me a copy of the updated report after completion of the entry.

When I moved my family to Florida from California, I notified ABC in Concord, California, of my move and new address. ABC continued to mail my statements to my old address in California. I notified ABC that I was not receiving my statements and that the statement had not been forwarded by the Post Office. It was over five months before I received a statement.

At that time, I did not realize that ABC was reporting my account as late and negative to the credit bureau. I offered to pay my account in full if ABC would remove the derogatory information from my credit report. It should never have been there in the first place.

Sincerely,


(Signature)


John Consumer

## 6.5 Sample Consumer Statement, #3

Name<br>
Address<br>
Soc. Sec<br>
Date of Birth<br>
City, State, Zip<br>
Date

Name of Credit Bureau
Street Address of Credit Bureau
City, State, Zip
via certified mail # xxxx xxxx

ATTN: CUSTOMER RELATIONS DEPARTMENT

Dear Sir or Madam,

Pursuant to the Fair Credit Reporting Act, Public Law 91-508, Title VI, Section 611 Sub Section B, I would like the following consumer statement added to my credit report.

On DATE, I moved to my present address. At that time, I notified all of my creditors, including NAME OF CREDITOR of my new address. NAME OF CREDITOR was very slow in changing my address on the monthly invoices to the correct one. As a result, several invoices were not received by me (and were not forwarded by the Post Office). The credit department at NAME OF CREDITOR made no effort to locate me, even though invoices were being returned to them. I notified NAME OF CREDITOR that I was not receiving their statements—it took them four weeks to figure out why! Upon receipt of all back-dated invoices, they were immediately paid in full. Unbeknownst to me, NAME OF CREDITOR was reporting my account as being late at the credit bureau. I first became aware of this when I went to apply for a car loan.

I have repeatedly asked the credit department at NAME OF CREDITOR to please clarify this misleading information on my credit report. Unfortunately, they have pursued this request with the same amount of efficiency, energy and zeal as they used to forward my mail to my correct address in the first place.

Please send me a copy of my updated credit report once the above has been completed. The above statement is most important to the unjust manner the above is presently being reflected on my credit report.

Your cooperation is greatly appreciated.

Sincerely,

Name

## 6.5 Sample Consumer Statement, #4

Name
Address
Soc. Sec. #
Date of Birth
City, State, Zip
Date

Name of Credit Bureau
Street Address of Credit Bureau
City, State, Zip
via certified mail # xxxx xxxx

Att: CUSTOMER RELATIONS DEPARTMENT

Dear Sir or Madam,

Pursuant to the Fair Credit Reporting Act, Public Law 91-508, Title VI, Section 611 Sub Section B, I would like the following consumer statement added to my credit report.

"Like most steel workers in our town, we were employed by NAME OF EMPLOYER. On DATE, 800 of us were laid off work for an indefinite period of time without any advance notice. During that time my wife stayed home with our newborn son; she was therefore not employed. We immediately became very concerned about our financial situation. Instead of avoiding our creditors, we chose to "take the bull by the horns" and contact all of them, including NAME OF CREDITOR and explain our predicament. As a result of our impeccable credit history, we were able to renegotiate all of our debt with all of our creditors with the exception of NAME OF CREDITOR. From the beginning, the credit department at NAME OF CREDITOR was extremely uncooperative to the point of being rude. Through hard work and determination, we have been able to pay off all of our debt as agreed in our renegotiated terms, including all amounts owed to NAME OF CREDITOR. Even though NAME OF CREDITOR has been paid in full, they still insist on reflecting this low period of income on my credit report."

Please send me a copy of my updated credit report once the above has been completed. The above statement is most important to the unjust manner the above is presently being reflected on my credit report.

Your cooperation is greatly appreciated.

Sincerely,

Name

6.6 Sample Dispute Letter, #1 (For items in credit reports that do not belong to the consumer, but to a former spouse.)

Name
Address
Soc. Sec. #
Date of Birth
City, State, Zip
Date

Name of Credit Bureau
Street Address of Credit Bureau
City, State, Zip
via certified mail # xxxx xxxx

Att: CUSTOMER RELATIONS DEPARTMENT

Dear Sir or Madam,

I am requesting that the following items listed below be immediately investigated. These items are not my account's or inquiries. They belong to my former spouse, and I would like them removed to reflect my true and accurate credit history. These inaccuracies are most injurious to my credit history.

Subscriber Name                  Subscriber #              Account #

Additionally, the following credit inquires were not authorized by me; I would like them removed.

Subscriber Name                  Subscriber #              Date of Inquiry

Please forward to me my updated credit report after you have completed your credit investigation.

Your cooperation in this matter is greatly appreciated.

Sincerely,


Name

6.6 Sample Dispute Letter, #2 (For items in credit reports that are inaccurately being reported.)

```
                                                                 Name
                                                              Address
                                                           Soc. Sec. #
                                                         Date of Birth
                                                                 Date


Name of Credit Bureau
Street Address of Credit Bureau
City, State, Zip
via certified mail # xxxx xxxx

ATT: CUSTOMER RELATIONS DEPARTMENT

Dear Sir or Madam,

I am in disagreement with the following items listed below which still appear on my
credit report, even after your investigation.  These incorrect items are highly injurious
to my credit rating and are not true.

Subscriber Name              Subscriber #   Acct # Reason why Incorrect

I would like the above listed immediately reinvestigated.  Furthermore, in accordance
with The Fair Credit Reporting Act, Public Law 91-508 Title VI, Section 611,
Subsection A-D, I would like the names and business addresses of each individual (s)
with whom you verified the above, so that I may follow up.

Please forward to me my updated credit report after you have completed your credit
investigation.

Your cooperation is greatly appreciated.

Yours Truly,



Name
```

6.6 Sample Dispute Letter, #3 (For items in credit reports that do not belong to the consumer.)

Name
Address
Soc. Sec. #
Date of Birth
City, State, Zip
Date

Name of Credit Bureau
Street Address of Credit Bureau
City, State, Zip
via certified mail # xxxx xxxx

ATT: CUSTOMER RELATIONS DEPARTMENT

Dear Sir or Madam,

I am requesting that the following items listed below be immediately investigated. These items are not my account's or inquiries and I would like them removed to reflect my true and accurate credit history. These inaccuracies are most injurious to my credit history.

Subscriber Name          Subscriber #          Account #

Additionally, the following credit inquires were not authorized by me; I would like them removed.

Subscriber Name          Subscriber #          Date of Inquiry

Please forward to me my updated credit report after you have completed your credit investigation.

Your cooperation in this matter is greatly appreciated.

Yours Truly,

Name

## 6.6 Sample Dispute Letter, #4 (Reporting accounts letter.)

Name<br>
Address<br>
Soc. Sec. #<br>
Date of Birth<br>
City, State, Zip<br>
Date

Name of Credit Bureau
Street Address of Credit Bureau
City, State, Zip
via certified mail # xxxx xxxx

ATT: CUSTOMER RELATIONS DEPARTMENT

Dear Sir or Madam,

At your earliest opportunity I would like you to please list the following credit references on my credit report.

Subscribe Name          Subscriber #          Account #

Will you please send me an updated credit report once the above has been completed. If there is any expense for this service, please advise.

Your Cooperation in this matter is greatly appreciated.

Yours Truly,

Name

6.6 Sample Dispute Letter, #5 (When you receive no response to a dispute letter.)

Name
Address
City, State, Zip
Soc. Sec. #
Date of Birth
Date

Name of Credit Bureau
Street Address of Credit Bureau
City, State, Zip
via certified mail # xxxx xxxx

ATT: CUSTOMER RELATIONS DEPARTMENT

Dear Sir or Madam:

On DATE LETTER WAS SENT, I sent you a letter requesting that several items be investigated on my credit report. (Please see enclosed copy).

As of yet I have not received a response from you. Under the Fair Credit Reporting Act you are required to respond within a "reasonable period of time"; please do so.

Yours Truly,

Name

6.6 Sample Dispute Letter, #6 (When you receive no response to a dispute letter.)

Name
Address
Social Security #
Date of Birth
City, State, Zip

Date

Name of Credit Bureau
Street Address of Credit Bureau
City, State, Zip
via certified mail # xxxx xxxx

ATTN: CUSTOMER RELATIONS DEPARTMENT

Dear Sir or Madam:

On date Letter I, II or III was sent, I sent you a letter requesting that several highly derogatory items which do not pertain to me, be investigated on my credit report (please see enclosed).

Additionally, on date Letter VIII was sent, I sent you a letter asking you to please expedite this investigation (please see enclosed). Since then, more than a reasonable amount of time has passed.

As of yet, I have not received a response to either one! Please be advised that unless my credit investigation is completed, I will file a formal complaint with the Federal Trade Commission. I hope this will not be necessary.

Yours truly,

(Your signature)

Name
Enclosures

6.6 Sample Dispute Letter, #7 (For items in credit reports that are inaccurately being reported.)

Name
Address
Social Security #
Date of Birth
City, State,. Zip

Date

Name of Credit Bureau
Street Address of Credit Bureau
City, State, Zip
via certified mail # xxxx xxxx

ATTN: CUSTOMER RELATIONS DEPARTMENT

Dear Sir or Madam:

I am requesting that the following items listed below be immediately investigated. These accounts have been paid promptly and satisfactorily and do not reflect my true and accurate credit history. These inaccuracies are extremely injurious and unfair to my credit history.

Subscriber Name          Subscriber #          Account #

Additionally, the following credit inquiries were not authorized by me, and I would like them removed.

Subscriber Name          Subscriber #          Date of Inquiry

Please forward to me an updated credit report after you have completed your credit investigation.

Your cooperation in this matter is greatly appreciated.

Yours truly,

(Your signature)
Name

## 6.6 Sample Dispute Letter, #8

Name
Address
Social Security #
Date of Birth
City, State, Zip

Date

Name of Credit Bureau
Street Address of Credit Bureau
City, State, Zip
via certified mail # xxxx xxxx

Dear Sir or Madam:

I am requesting that the accounts and subscribers I have identified below be investigated as these are not my accounts and I wish to have them removed to reflect my excellent credit rating.

| SUBSCRIBER | SUBSCRIBER # | ACCOUNT # |
|---|---|---|
| XYZ    Store<br>CURWAS 30-4 10-77 | 934754545 | |
| BOA<br>PD CHG OFF 7-80 | 934714535 | |

Would you please forward to me an updated credit report after the completion of your investigations.

Yours truly,

(Your signature)

Name

## 6.6 Sample Dispute Letter, #9

Name
Address
Social Security #
Date of Birth
City, State, Zip
Date

Name of Credit Bureau
Street Address
City, State, Zip
via certified mail # xxxx xxxx

Dear Sir or Madam:

Would you please investigate the status of the account I have listed below, as I have paid it satisfactorily.

| SUBSCRIBER | SUBSCRIBER # | ACCOUNT # |
| --- | --- | --- |
| XYZ    Savings
Current Account $500 | 1929302 | |

Would you also please reinvestigate the inquiries for credit I have listed below as I wish to determine the accuracy of the information contained on my credit report. These inquiries are extremely injurious to my credit history.

| | | |
| --- | --- | --- |
| XYZ Store
Inquiry | 37283828 | |
| SPNB
Inquiry 3-30-82 | 39289302 | |

After your investigation, would you please forward to me an updated copy of my credit report.

Yours truly,

(Your Signature)
Name

## 6.6 Sample Dispute Letter, #10

Name
Address
Social Security #
Date of Birth
City, State, Zip

Date

Name of Credit Bureau
Street Address
City, State, Zip
via certified mail # xxxx xxxx

Dear Sir or Madam:

I recently received a copy of the report containing my credit history and I disagree with the following information.

| | | |
|---|---|---|
| City Dept. Store | AN 505204638 | Information on my report is incorrect. |
| XYZ Bank | AN 528392899 | This is not my account. |
| ABC Bank | AN 102938490 | I was never 90 days late on this account. |

Under the Fair Credit Reporting Act, I understand that the information I have disputed will be rechecked at the source, and I will be notified of the results of this recheck within days. I also want the names and business addresses of the personnel you checked with at each company, so that I can follow up (Fair Credit Reporting Act, Public Law 91-508 Title IV, Section 611, Sub-section A through D.)

Yours truly,

(Your signature)

Name

## 6.7 Complaint Letter - Bank #1

Name
Address
City, State, Zip
Work phone number
Home phone number
Date

Director, Division of Consumer Affairs          Ref: Name of Bank
Board of Governors of the                       Address
Federal Reserve System                          City, State, Zip
Washington, DC 20551                            Acct. # (if applicable)
via certified mail # xxxx xxxx

Dear Sir or Madam:

Please accept this letter as a formal complaint on the above-referenced bank. My complaint is as follows:


        (Your information here)


I have tried to resolve the above-described problem directly with NAME OF BANK, but to no avail. The key person I dealt with was NAME OF PERSON WITH WHOM YOU DEALT.

I have enclosed photo copies of all pertinent paperwork to document my claims.

Yours truly,

(Your signature)

Name
Enclosures.

## 6.7 Complaint Letter - Bank, #2

Name
Address
City, State, Zip
Work phone number
Home phone number

Date

Controller of the Currency                      Ref: Name of Bank
Consumer Affairs Division                       Address
Washington, DC 20219                            City, State, Zip
via certified mail # xxxx xxxx                  Acct. # (if applicable)

Dear Sir or Madam:

Please accept this letter as a formal complaint on the above referenced bank. My complaint is as follows:

    (Your complaint would be entered here)

I have tried to resolve the above-described problem directly with NAME OF BANK to no avail. The key person I dealt with was NAME OF PERSON WITH WHOM YOU DEALT.

I have enclosed photo copies of all pertinent paperwork to document my claims.

Yours truly,

(Your signature)

Name

## 6.7 Complaint Letters - Bank, #3

Name
Address
City, State, Zip

Work phone number
Home phone number

Federal Deposit Insurance Corporation
Office of Customer Affairs
Washington, DC 20429
via certified mail # xxxx xxxx

Date

Ref: Name of Bank
Address
City, State, Zip

Account # (if possible)

Dear Sir or Madam:

Please accept this letter as a formal complaint on the above-referenced bank. My complaint is as follows:

(Your complaint is entered here)

I have tried to resolve the above-described problem directly with NAME OF BANK, but to no avail. The key person with whom I dealt with was NAME OF PERSON WITH WHOM YOU DEALT.

I have enclosed photo copies of all pertinent paperwork to document my claims.

Sincerely,

(Your signature)

Name

## 6.8 Reported Accounts Letter

Name
Address
City, State, Zip

Date


Any Credit Bureau
Street Address
Anytown, State, Zip
via certified mail # xxxx xxxx

Dear Sir or Madam:

I am requesting that the subscribers listed here report these accounts on my credit report. I would like these accounts to be entered on my credit file to further build my good credit rating.

| SUBSCRIBER | SUBSCRIBER # | ACCOUNT # |
|---|---|---|
| ROBINSONS CURRENT ACCOUNT | B83857892 | |
| BROADWAY | 83481782 | |

Would you please forward to me an updated credit report after the completion of your investigation.

Sincerely,

(Your signature)

John Consumer
SS #

## 6.9 Cease Collection Letter

Your Name
Address
City, State, Zip


Date


Mr. John Smith, President
ABC Collection Company
123 Main Street
City, State, Zip
via certified mail # xxxx xxxx

Dear Sir or Madam:

Pursuant to the Fair Debt Collection Practices Act, I hereby direct you to cease further communications regarding the alleged Bloomingdale's debt of $89.00.

Any further communications or collection efforts, except those specifically permitted by law, will constitute an unlawful act punishable by up to $1,000 in civil action damages, plus attorney's fees, and/or Federal Trade Commission penalties of up to $10,000 per day for such violation.

Sincerely,

(Your signature)

Name
cc: Bloomingdale's

VIA CERTIFIED MAIL, RETURN RECEIPT REQUESTED

## 6.10 Same Request Letter (Credit Bureau Decoding Department)

Name
Address
Social Security #
Date of Birth
City, State, Zip

Date

Name of Credit Bureau
Street Address of Credit Bureau
City, State, Zip
via certified mail # xxxx xxxx

ATTN: DECODING DEPARTMENT

Dear Sir or Madam:

At your first opportunity, will you please provide me with the names, addresses and telephone numbers of the following subscribers:

SUBSCRIBER             SUBSCRIBER #              DATE OF REPORT

These subscribers have run unauthorized credit reports on me (please see enclosed credit report) and I wish to contact them to inquire why.

Your cooperation is greatly appreciated.

Yours truly,

(Your signature)

Name
Enclosures

# CHAPTER 7

## LEGISLATION DEALING WITH CREDIT

O n the following pages in this chapter, we have included copies of the laws and regulations that deal with the issues we've been discussing in this manual:

**The Fair Credit Reporting Act**
**Public Law 91-508 effective April 25, 1971 and Amendments**
**(15 U.S.C. § 1681 et seq.)**

**TITLE VI-PROVISIONS RELATING TO CREDIT REPORTING AGENCIES**
**AMENDMENT OF CONSUMER CREDIT PROTECTION ACT**

*Sec. 601. The Consumer Credit Protection Act is amended by adding at the end thereof of the following new title;*

**TITLE VI-CONSUMER CREDIT REPORTING**

**Sec**

# § 601. Short title

"This Title may be cited as the Fair Credit Reporting Act.

## § 602. Findings and purpose

(a) The congress makes the following findings:

"(1) The banking system is dependent upon fair and accurate credit reporting. Inaccurate credit report directly undermine the public confidence which is essential to the continued functioning of the banking system.

"(2) An elaborate mechanism has been developed for investigating and evaluating the credit worthiness, credit standing, credit capacity, character, and general reputation of consumer.

"(3) Consumer reporting agencies have assumed a vital role in assembling and evaluating consumer credit and other information on consumers.

"(4) There is a need to insure that consumer reporting agencies exercise their grave responsibilities with fairness, impartiality, and a respect for the consumer's right to privacy.

"(b) It is the purpose of this title to require that consumer reporting agencies adopt reasonable procedures for meeting the needs of commerce for consumer credit, personnel, insurance, and other information in a manner which is fair and equitable to the consumer, with regard to the confidentiality, accuracy, relevancy, and proper utilization of such information in accordance with the requirements of this title.

## § 603. Definitions and rules of construction

"(a) Definitions and rules of construction set forth in this section are applicable for the purposes of this title.

"(b) The term 'person' means any individual, partnership, corporation, trust estate, cooperative, association, government or governmental subdivision or agency, or other entity.

"(c) The term 'consumer' means an individual.

"(d) The term 'consumer report' means any written, oral, or other communication of any information by a consumer reporting agency bearing on a consumer's credit worthiness, credit standing, credit capacity, character, general reputation, personal characteristics, or mode of living which is used or expected to be used or collected in whole or in part for the purpose of serving as a factor in establishing the consumer's eligibility for (1) credit or insurance to be used primarily for personal, family, or household purposes, or (2) employment purposes, or (3) other purposes authorized under section 604. The term does not include (A) any report containing information solely as to transactions or experiences between the consumer and the person making the report; (B) any authorization or approval of a specific extension of credit directly or indirectly by the issuer of a credit card or similar device; or (C) any report in which a person who has been requested by a third party to make a specific extension of credit directly or indirectly to a consumer conveys his decision with respect to such request, if the third party advises the consumer of the name and address of the person to whom the request the request was made and such person makes the disclosure to the consumer required under section 615.

"(e) The term 'investigative consumer report' means a consumer report or portion thereof in which information on a consumer's character, general reputation, personal characteristics, or mode of living is obtained through personal interviews with neighbors, friends, or associates of the consumer reported on or with others with whom he is acquainted or who may have knowledge concerning any such items of information. However, such information shall not include specific factual information on a consumer's credit record obtained directly from a creditor of the consumer or from a consumer reporting agency when such information was obtained directly from a creditor of the consumer or from the consumer.

"(f) The term 'consumer reporting agency' means any person which, for monetary fees, dues, or on a cooperative nonprofit basis, regularly engages in whole or in part in the practice of assembling or evaluating consumer reports to third parties, and which uses any means or facility of interstate commerce for the preparing or furnishing consumer reports.

"(g) The term 'file', when used in connection with information on any consumer, means all of the information on that consumer recorded and retained by a consumer reporting agency regardless of how the information is stored.

"(h) The term 'employment purposes' when used in connection with a consumer report means a report used for the purpose of evaluating a consumer for employment, promotion, reassignment, or retention as an employee.

"(i)The term 'medical information 'means information or records obtained, with the consent of the individual to whom it relates, from licensed physicians or medical practitioners, hospitals, clinics, or other medical or medically related facilities.

### § 604. Permissible purposes of reports

"A consumer reporting agency may furnish a consumer report under the following circumstances and no other:

"(1) In response to the order of a court having jurisdiction to issue such an order, or a subpoena issued in connection with proceedings before a Federal grand jury.

"(2) In accordance with the written instructions of the consumer to whom it relates.

"(3) To a person which it has reason to believe-

"(A) intends to use the information in connection with a credit transaction involving the consumer on whom the information is to be furnished and involving the extension of credit to, or review or collection of an account of, the consumer; or

"(B) intends to use the information for employment purposes;  or

"(C)intends to use the information in connection with the underwriting of insurance involving the consumer; or

"(D) intends to use the information in connection with a determination of the consumer's eligibility for  a license or other benefit granted by a governmental instrumentality required by law to consider an applicant's financial responsibility or status; or

"(E) otherwise has a legitimate business need for the information in connection with a business transaction involving the consume.

### § 605. Obsolete information

"(a) Except as authorized under subsection (b), no consumer reporting agency may make any consumer report containing any of the following items of information:

"(1) Case under title 11 of the United States Code or under the Bankruptcy Act that, from the date of entry of the order for relief or the date of adjudication, as the cause may be, antedate the report by more than 10 years.

"(2) Suits and judgments which, from date of entry, antedate the report by more than seven years or until the governing statute of limitations has expired, whichever is the longer period.

"(3) Paid tax liens which, from date of payment, antedate the report by more than seven years.

"(4) Accounts placed for collection or charged to profit and loss which antedate the report by more than seven years.

"(5) Records of arrest, indictment, or conviction of crime which, from date of disposition, release, or parole, antedate the report by more than seven years.

"(6) Any other adverse item of information which antedates the report by more than seven years.

"(b) The provisions of subsection (a) are not applicable in the case of any consumer credit report to be used in connection with-

"(1) a credit transaction involving, or which may reasonably be expected to involve, a principal amount of $50,000 or more;

"(2) the underwriting of life insurance involving, or which may reasonably be expected to involve, a face amount of $50,000 or more; or

"(3) the employment of any individual at an annual salary which equals, or which may reasonably be expected to equal $20,000, or more.

20 U.S.C. 1080a(f)-Referencing Federally Guaranteed Student Loans

Notwithstanding paragraphs (4) and (6) of subsection (a) of section 605 of the Fair Credit Reporting Act (15 U.S.C. §§ 1681c(a)(4), (a)(6)), a consumer reporting agency may make a report containing information received from the Secretary or a guaranty agency, eligible lender, or subsequent holder regarding the status of a borrower's defaulted account on a loan guaranteed under this part {20 USCS §§ 1071 et seq.} until-

(1) 7 years from the date on which the Secretary or the agency paid a claim to the holder on the guaranty,

(2) 7 years from the date the Secretary, guaranty agency, eligible lender, or subsequent holder first reported the account to the consumer reporting agency; or

(3) in the case of a borrower who reenters repayment after defaulting on a loan and subsequently goes into default on such loan, 7 years from the date the loan entered default such subsequent time.

## § 606. Disclosure of investigative consumer reports

"(a) A person may not procure or cause to be prepared an investigative consumer report on any consumer unless-

"(1) it is clearly and accurately disclosed to the consumer that an investigative consumer report including information as to his character, general reputation, personal characteristics, and mode of living, whichever are applicable, may be made, and such disclosure (A) is made in a writing mailed, or otherwise delivered, to the consumer, not later than three days after the date on which the report was first requested , and (B) includes a statement informing the consumer of his right to request the addition- al disclosures provided for under subsection (b) of this section; or

"(2) the report is to be used for employment purposes for which the consumer has not specifically applied.

"(b) Any person who procures or causes to be prepared an investigative consumer report on any consumer shall, upon written request made by the consumer within a reasonable period of time after the receipt by him of the disclosure required by subsection (a)(1), shall make a complete and accurate disclosure of the nature and scope of the investigation requested. This Disclosure shall be made in a writing mailed, or otherwise delivered, to the consumer not later than five days after the date on which the request for such disclosure was received from the consumer or such report was first requested, whichever is the later.

"(c) No person may be held liable for any violation of subsection (a) or (b) of this section if he shows by a preponderance of the evidence that at the time of the violation he maintained reasonable procedures to assure compliance with subsection (a) or (b).

## § 607. Compliance procedures

"(a) Every consumer reporting agency shall maintain reasonable procedures designed to avoid violations of section 605 and to limit the furnishing of consumer reports to the purposes listed under section 604. These procedures shall require that prospective users of the information identify themselves, certify the purposes for which the information is sought, and certify that the information will be used for no other purpose. Every consumer reporting agency shall make a reasonable effort to verify the identity of a new prospective user and the uses certified by such prospective user prior to furnishing such user a consumer report. No consumer reporting agency may furnish a consumer report to any person if it has reasonable grounds for believing that the consumer report will not be used for a purpose listed in section 604.

"(b) Whenever a consumer reporting agency prepares a consumer report it shall follow reasonable procedures to assure maximum possible accuracy of the information concerning the individual about whom the report relates.

### § 608. Disclosures to governmental agencies

"Notwithstanding the provisions of section 604, a consumer reporting agency may furnish identifying information respecting any consumer, limited to his name, address, former addresses, places of employment, or former places of employment, to a governmental agency.

### § 609. Disclosures to consumers

"(a) Every consumer reporting agency shall, upon request and proper identification of any consumer, clearly and accurately disclose to the consumer:

"(1) The nature and substance of all information (except medical information) in its files on the consumer at the time of the request.

"(2) The sources of the information; except that the sources of information acquired solely for use in preparing an investigative consumer report and actually used for no other purpose need not be disclosed: Provided, That in the event an action is brought under this title, such sources shall be avail- able to the plaintiff under appropriate discovery procedures in the court in which the action is brought.

"(3) The recipients of any consumer report on the consumer which it has furnished-

"(A) for employment purposes within the two-year period preceding the request, and

"(B) for any other purpose within the six-month period preceding the request.

"(4) The dates, original payees, and amounts of any checks upon which is based any adverse characterization of the consumer, included in the file at the time of the disclosure.

"(b) The requirements of subsection (a) respecting the disclosure of sources of information and the recipients of consumer reports do not apply to information received or consumer reports furnished prior to the effective date of this title except to the extent that the matter involved is contained in the files of the consumer reporting agency on that date.

### § 610. Conditions of disclosure to consumers

"(a) A consumer reporting agency shall make the disclosures required under section 609 during normal business hours and on reasonable notice.

"(b) The disclosures required under section 609 shall be made to the consumer-

"(1) in person if he appears in person and furnishes proper identification; or

"(2) by telephone if he has made a written request, with proper identification, for telephone disclosure and the tool charge, if any, for the telephone call is prepaid by or charged directly to the consumer.

"(c) Any consumer reporting agency shall provide trained personnel to explain to the consumer any information furnished to him pursuant to section 609.

"(d) The consumer shall be permitted to be accompanied by one other person of his choosing, who shall furnish reasonable identification. A consumer reporting agency may require the consumer to furnish a written statement granting permission to the consumer reporting agency to discuss the con- sumer's file in such person's presence.

"(e) Except as provided in sections 616 and 617, no consumer may bring any action or proceeding in the nature of defamation, invasion of privacy, or negligence with respect to the reporting of information against any consumer reporting agency, any user of information, or any person who furnishes information to a consumer reporting agency, based on information disclosed pursuant to sections 609, 610 or 615, except as to false information furnished with malice willful intent to injure such con- sumer.

## § 611. Procedure in case of disputed accuracy

"(a) If the completeness or accuracy of any item of information contained in his file is disputed by a consumer, and such dispute is directly conveyed to the consumer reporting agency by the consumer, the consumer reporting agency shall within a reasonable period of time reinvestigate and record the current status of that information unless it has reasonable grounds to believe that the dispute by the consumer is frivolous or irrelevant. If after such reinvestigation such information is found to be inac- curate or can no longer be verified, the consumer reporting agency shall promptly delete such infor- mation. The presence of contradictory information in the consumer's file does not in and of itself con- stitute reasonable grounds for believing the dispute is frivolous or irrelevant.

"(b) If the reinvestigation does not resolve the dispute, the consumer may file a brief statement setting forth the nature of the dispute. The consumer reporting agency may limit such statement to not more than one hundred words if it provides the consumer with assistance in writing a clear summary of the dispute.

"(c) Whenever a statement of a dispute is filed, unless there is reasonable grounds to believe that it is frivolous or irrelevant, the consumer reporting agency shall, in any subsequent consumer report con- taining the information in question, clearly note that it is disputed by the consumer and provide either the consumer's statement or a clear and accurate codification or summary thereof.

"(d) Following any deletion of information which is found to be inaccurate or whose accuracy can no longer be verified or any notation as to disputed information, the consumer reporting agency shall, at the request of the consumer, furnish notification that the item has been deleted or the statement, cod- ification or summary pursuant to subsection (b) or (c) to any person specifically designated by the con- sumer who has within two years prior thereto received a consumer report for employment purposes, or within six months prior thereto received a consumer report for any other purpose, which contained the deleted or disputed information. The consumer reporting agency shall clearly and conspicuously disclose to the consumer his rights to make such a request. Such disclosure shall be made at or prior to the time the information is deleted or the consumer's statement regarding the disputed information is received.

## § 612. Charges for certain disclosures

"A consumer reporting agency shall make all disclosures pursuant to section 609 and furnish all con- sumer reports pursuant to section 611(d) without charge to the consumer if, within thirty days after receipt by such consumer of a notification pursuant to section 615 or notification from a debt collection agency affiliated with such consumer reporting agency stating that the consumer's credit rating may be or has been adversely affected, the consumer makes a request under section 609 or 611(d). Otherwise, the consumer reporting agency may impose a reasonable charge on the consumer for making disclosure to such consumer pursuant to section 609, the charge for which shall be indicated to the consumer prior to making disclosure; and for furnishing notifications, statements, summaries, or codifications to person designated by the consumer pursuant to section 611(d), the charge for which shall be indicated to the consumer prior to furnishing such information and shall not exceed the charge that the consumer reporting agency would impose on each designated recipient for a con- sumer report except that no charge may be made for notifying such persons of the deletion of infor- mation which is found to be inaccurate or which can no longer verified.

## § 613. Public record information for employment purpose

"A consumer reporting agency which furnishes a consumer report for employment purposes and which for that purpose compiles and reports items of information on consumers which are matters of public record and are likely to have an adverse effect upon a consumer's ability to obtain employment shall-

"(1) at the time such public record information is reported to the user of such consumer report, notify the consumer of the fact that public record information is being reported by the consumer reporting agency, together with the name and address of the person to whom such information is being reported; or

"(2) maintain strict procedures designed to ensure that whenever public record information which is likely to have an adverse effect on a consumer's ability to obtain employment is reported it is complete and up to date. For purposes of this paragraph, items of public record relating to arrests, indictment, conviction, suits, tax liens, and outstanding judgments shall be considered up to date if the cur- rent public record status of the item at the time of the report is reported.

### § 614. Restrictions on investigative consumer report

"Whenever a consumer reporting agency prepares an investigative consumer report, no adverse information in the consumer report (other than information which is a matter of public record) may be included in a subsequent consumer report unless such adverse information has been verified in the process of making such subsequent consumer report, or the adverse information was received with- in the three-month period preceding the date the subsequent report is furnished.

### § 615. Requirement on users of consumer report

"(a) Whenever credit or insurance for personal, family, or household purposes, or employment involving a consumer is denied or the charge for such credit or insurance is increased either wholly or partly because of information contained in a consumer report from a consumer reporting agency, the user of the consumer report shall so advise the consumer against whom such adverse action has been taken and supply the name and address of the consumer reporting agency making the report.

"(b)Whenever credit for personal, family, or household purposes involving a consumer is denied or the charge for such credit is increased either wholly or partly because of information obtained from a person other than a consumer reporting agency bearing upon the consumer's credit worthiness, credit standing, credit capacity, character, general reputation, personal characteristics, or mode of living, the user of such information shall, within a reasonable period of time, upon the consumer's written request for the reasons for such adverse action received within sixty days after learning of such adverse action, disclose the nature of the information to the consumer. The user of such information shall clearly and accurately disclose to the consumer his right to make such written request at the time such adverse action is communicated to the consumer.

"(c) No person shall be held liable for any violation of this section if he shows by a preponderance of the of the evidence that at the time of alleged violation he maintained reasonable procedures to assure compliance with the provisions of subsections (a) and (b).

### "§ 616. Civil liability for willful noncompliance

"Any consumer reporting agency or user of information which willfully fails to comply with any requirement imposed under this title with respect to any consumer is liable to that consumer in an amount equal to the sum of-

"(1) any actual damages sustained by the consumer as a result of the failure;

"(2) such amount of punitive damages as the court may allow; and

"(3) in the case of any successful action to enforce any liability under this section, the costs of the action together with reasonable attorney's fees as determined by the court.

### § 617. Civil liability for negligent noncompliance

"Any consumer reporting agency or user of information which is negligent in failing to comply with any requirement imposed under this title with respect to any consumer is liable to that consumer in an amount equal to the sum of-

"(1) any actual damages sustained by the consumer as a result of the failure.

"(2) in the case of any successful action to enforce any liability under this section, the costs of the action together with reasonable attorney's fees as determined by the court.

### § 618. Jurisdiction of courts; limitation of actions

" An action to enforce any liability created under this title may be brought in any appropriate United States district court without regard to the amount in controversy, or in any other court of competent jurisdiction, within two years from the date on which the liability arises, except that where a defendant has materially and willfully misrepresented any information required under this title to be disclosed to an individual and the information so misrepresented is material to the establishment of the defendant's liability to that individual under this title, the action may be brought at any time within two years after discovery by the individual of the misrepresentation.

### § 619. Obtaining information under false pretenses

"Any person who knowingly and willfully obtains information on a consumer from a consumer reporting agency under false pretenses shall be fined not more than $5,000 or imprisoned not more than one year, or both.

### § 620. Unauthorized disclosures by officers or employees

"Any officer or employee of a consumer reporting agency who knowingly and willfully provides information concerning an individual from the agency's files to a person not authorized to receive that information shall be fined not more than $5,000 or imprisoned not more than one year, or both.

### § 621. Administrative enforcement

"(a) Compliance with the requirements imposed under this title shall be enforced under the Federal Trade Commission Act by the Federal Trade Commission with respect to consumer reporting agencies and all other persons subject thereto, except to the extent that enforcement of the requirements imposed under this title is specifically committed to some other government agency under subsection (b) hereof. For the purpose of the exercise by the Federal Trade Commission of its functions and powers under the Federal Trade Commission Act, a violation of any requirement or prohibition imposed under this title shall constitute an unfair or deceptive act or practice in commerce in violation of section 5(a) of the Federal Trade Commission Act and shall be subject to enforcement by the Federal Trade Commission under section 5(b) thereof with respect to any consumer reporting agency or per- son subject to enforcement by the Federal Trade Commission pursuant to this subsection, irrespective of whether that person is engaged in commerce or meets any other jurisdictional tests in the Federal Trade Commission Act. The Federal Trade Commission shall have such procedural, investigative, and enforcement powers, including the power to issue procedural rules in enforcing compliance with the requirements imposed under this title and the appearance of witnesses as though the applicable terms and conditions of the Federal Trade Commission Act were part of this title. Any per- son violating any of the provisions of this title shall be subject to the penalties and entitled to the privileges and immunities provided in the Federal Trade Commission Act as though the applicable terms and provisions thereof were part of this title.

"(b) Compliance with the requirement imposed under this title with respect to consumer reporting agencies and persons who use consumer reports from such agencies shall be enforced

"(1) section 8 of the Federal Deposit Insurance Act, in the case of:

"(A) national banks, by the Comptroller of the Currency.

"(B) member banks of the Federal Reserve System (other than national banks), by the Federal Reserve Board; and

"(C)banks insured by the Federal Deposit Insurance Corporation (other than members of the Federal Reserve System), by the Board of Directors of the Federal Deposit Insurance Corporation.

"(2) section 8 of the Federal Deposit Insurance Act (12 USCS § 1818), by the Director of the Office of Thrift Supervision, in the case of a savings association the deposits of which are insured by the Federal Deposit Insurance Corporation;

"(3) the Federal Credit Union Act, by the Administrator of the National Credit Union Administration with respect to any Federal credit union.

"(4) the Acts to regulate commerce, by the Secretary of Transportation, with respect to any air carrier subject to the jurisdiction of the Surface |Transportation Board.

"(5) the Federal Aviation Act of 1958, by the Civil Aeronautics Board with respect to any air carrier or foreign air carrier subject to that Act; and

"(6) The Packers and Stockyards Act, 1912 (except as provided in section 406 of that Act), by the Secretary of Agriculture with respect to any activities subject to that Act.

"(c) For the purpose of the exercise by any agency referred to in subsection (b) of its powers under any Act referred to in that subsection, a violation of any requirements imposed under this title shall be deemed to be a violation of a requirement imposed under that Act. In addition to its powers under any provision of law specifically referred to in subsection (b), each of the agencies referred to in that subsection may exercise for the purpose of enforcing compliance with any requirement imposed under this title any other authority conferred on it by law.

## § 622. Information on overdue child support obligations

Notwithstanding any other provision of this title (15 USCS §§ 1681 et seq.), a consumer reporting agency shall include in any consumer report furnished by the agency in accordance with section 604 (15 USCS §1681b), any information on the failure of the consumer to pay overdue support which-

(1)is provided-

    (A) to the consumer reporting agency by a State or local child support enforcement agency; or

    (B) to the consumer reporting agency and verified by any local, State, or Federal Government agency; and

(2)antedates the report by 7 years or less.

## § 623. Relation to State laws

"This title does not annul, alter, affect, or exempt any person subject to the provisions of this title from complying with the laws of any State with respect to the collection, distribution, or use of any information on consumers, except to the extent that those law are inconsistent with any provision of this title, and then only to the extent of the inconsistency."

## § 624. Disclosures to FBI for counterintelligence purposes

"(a) Identity of Financial Institutions. Notwithstanding section 604 or any other provision of this title, a consumer reporting agency shall furnish to the Federal Bureau of Investigation the names and addresses of all financial institutions (as that term is defined in section 1101 of The Right to Financial Privacy Act of 1978) at which a consumer maintains or has maintained an account, to the extent that informadion is in the files of the agency, when presented with a written request for that information, signed by the Director of the Federal Bureau of Investigation, or the Director's designee, which certifies compliance with this section. The Director or the Director' designee may make such a certification only if the Director or the Director's designee has determined in writing that-

"(1) such information is necessary for the conduct of an authorized foreign counterintelligence investigation; and

"(2) there are specific and articulable facts giving reason to believe that the consumer-

"(A) is a foreign power (as defined in section 101 of The Foreign Intelligence Surveillance Act of 1978) or a person who is not a United States person (as defined in such section 101) and is an official of a foreign power; or

"(B) is an agent of a foreign power and is engaging or has engaged in act if international terrorism (as that term is defined in section 101 (C) of The Foreign Intelligence Surveillance Act of 1978) or clandestine intelligence activities that involve or may involve a violation of criminal of The United States.

"(b) Identifying Information. Notwithstanding the provisions of section 604 or any other provision of this title, a consumer reporting agency shall furnish identifying information respecting a consumer, limited to name, address, former address, places of employment, or former places of employment, to the Federal Bureau of Investigation when presented with a written request, signed by the Director or the Director' designee, which certifies compliance with the subsection. The Director or the Director's designee may take such a certification only if the Director or the Director's designee has determined in writing that-

"(1) such information is necessary to the conduct of an authorized counterintelligence investigation; and

"(2) there is information giving reason to believe that the consumer has been, or is about to be, in contact with the foreign power or an agent of a foreign power (as defined in section 101 of The Foreign Intelligence Surveillance Act of 1978).

"(c) Court Order for Disclosure of Consumer Reports. Notwithstanding section 604 or any other provision of this title, if requested in writing by the Director of the Federal Bureau of Investigation, or designee of the Director, a court may issue an order ex parte directing a consumer reporting agency to furnish a consumer report to the Federal Bureau of Investigation, upon a showing in a camera that-

"(1) the consumer report is necessary for the conduct of an authorized foreign counterintelligence investigation; and

"(2) there are specific and articulable facts giving reason to believe that the consumer whose con- sumer report is sought-

"(A)is an agent of a foreign power, and

"(B) is engaging or has engaged in act of international terrorism (as that term is defined in section 101 (c) of the Foreign Intelligence Surveillance Act of 1978) or clandestine intelligence activities that involve or may involve a violation of criminal statutes of the United States. The terms of an order issued under this subsection shall not disclose that the order is issued for purposes of a counterintelligence investigation.

"(d) Confidentiality. No consumer reporting agency or officer, employee, or agent of a consumer reporting agency shall disclose to any person, other than those officers, employees, or agents of a consumer reporting agency necessary to fulfill the requirement to disclose information to the Federal Bureau Investigation under this section, that the Federal Bureau of Investigation has sought or obtained the identity of financial institutions or consumer report respecting any consumer under the subsection (a), (b), or (c), and no consumer reporting agency or officer, employee, or agent of a con- sumer reporting agency shall include in any consumer report any information that would indicate that the Federal Bureau of Investigation has sought or obtained such information or a consumer report.

"(e) Payment of Fees. The Federal Bureau of Investigation shall, subject to the availability of appropriations, pay to the consumer reporting agency assembling or providing report or information in accordance with procedures established under this section a fee for reimbursement for such costs as are reasonably necessary and which have been directly incurred in searching, reproducing, or transporting books, papers, records, or other data required or requested to be produced under this section.

"(f) Limit on Dissemination. The Federal Bureau of Investigation may not disseminate information obtained pursuant to this section outside of the Federal Bureau of Investigation, except to other federal agencies as may be necessary for the approval or conduct of a foreign counterintelligence investigation, or, where the information concerns a person subject to the Uniform Code of Military Justice, to appropriate investigative authorities within the military department concerned as may be necessary for the conduct of a joint foreign counterintelligence investigations.

"(g) Rules of Construction. Nothing in this section shall be construed to prohibit information from being furnished by the Federal Bureau of Investigation pursuant to a subpoena or court order, in connection with a judicial or administrative proceeding to enforce the provisions of this act. Nothing in this section shall be construed to authorize or permit the withholding of information from the Congress.

"(h) Reports to Congress. On a semiannual basis, the Attorney General shall fully inform the Permanent Select Committee on Intelligence and the Committee on Banking, Finance and Urban Affairs of the House of Representatives, and the select committee on Intelligence and Committee on Banking, Housing, and Urban Affairs of the Senate concerning all requests made pursuant to subsections (a), (b), and (c).

"(i) Damages. Any agency or department of the United States obtaining or disclosing any consumer reports, records, or information contained therein in violation of this section is liable to the consumer to whom such reports, records, or information relate in an amount equal to the sum of-

"(1) $100, without regard to the volume of consumer reports, records, or information involved;

"(2) any actual damages sustained by the consumer as a result for the disclosure;

"(3) if the violation is found to have been willful or intentional, such punitive damages as a court may allow; and

"(4) in the case of any successful action to enforce liability under this subsection, the costs of the action, together with reasonable attorney fees, as determined by the court.

"(j) Disciplinary Actions for Violations. If a court determines that any agency or department of the United States has violated any provision of this section and the court finds that the circumstances sur- rounding the violation raise questions of whether or not an officer or employee of the agency or department acted willfully or intentionally with respect to the violation, the agency or department shall promptly initiate a proceeding to determine whether or not disciplinary action is warranted against the officer or employee who was responsible for the violation.

"(k) Good-Faith Exception. Notwithstanding any other provision of this title, any consumer reporting agency or agent or employee thereof making disclosure of consumer reports or identifying information pursuant to this subsection in good-faith reliance upon a certification of the Federal Bureau of Investigation pursuant to this provisions of this section shall not be liable to any person for such disclosure under this title, the constitution of any state, or any laws or regulation of any state or any political of any state.

"(l) Limitation of Remedies. Notwithstanding any other provision of this title, the remedies and sanctions set forth in this section shall be the only judicial remedies and sanction for violation of this section.

"(m) Injunctive Relief. In addition to any other remedy contained in this section, injunctive relief shall be available to require compliance with the procedures of this section. In the event of any successful action under this subsection, costs together with reasonable attorney fees, as determined by the court, may be covered.".

This section 624 was added by amendment effective on January 6, 1996. This section 624 was added by amendment effective on January 6, 1996.

# A Summary of Your Rights
# Under the Fair Credit Reporting Act

The federal Fair Credit Reporting Act (FCRA) is designed to promote accuracy, fairness, and privacy of information in the files of every "consumer reporting agency" (CRA). Most CRAs are credit bureaus that gather and sell information about you — such as if you pay your bills on time or have filed bankruptcy — to creditors, employers, landlords, and other businesses. You can find the complete text of the FCRA, 15 U.S.C. §§1681-1681u. The FCRA gives you specific rights, as outlined below. You may have additional rights under state law. You may contact a state or local consumer protection agency or a state attorney general to learn those rights.

- **You must be told if information in your file has been used against you.** Anyone who uses information from a CRA to take action against you — such as denying an application for credit, insurance, or employment — must tell you, and give you the name, address, and phone number of the CRA that provided the consumer report.

- **You can find out what is in your file.** At your request, a CRA must give you the information in your file, and a list of everyone who has requested it recently. There is no charge for the report if a person has taken action against you because of information supplied by the CRA, if you request the report within 60 days of receiving notice of the action. You also are entitled to one free report every twelve months upon request if you certify that (1) you are unemployed and plan to seek employment within 60 days, (2) you are on welfare, or (3) your report is inaccurate due to fraud. Otherwise, a CRA may charge you up to eight dollars.

- **You can dispute inaccurate information with the CRA.** If you tell a CRA that your file contains inaccurate information, the CRA must investigate the items (usually within 30 days) by presenting to its information source all relevant evidence you submit, unless your dispute is frivolous. The source must review your evidence and report its findings to the CRA. (The source also must advise national CRAs — to which it has provided the data — of any error.) The CRA must give you a written report of the investigation, and a copy of your report if the investigation results in any change. If the CRA's investigation does not resolve the dispute, you may add a brief statement to your file. The CRA must normally include a summary of your statement in future reports. If an item is deleted or a dispute statement is filed, you may ask that anyone who has recently received your report be notified of the change.

- **Inaccurate information must be corrected or deleted.** A CRA must remove or correct inaccurate or unverified information from its files, usually within 30 days after you dispute it. **However, the CRA is not required to remove accurate data from your file unless it is outdated (as described below) or cannot be verified.** If your dispute results in any change to your report, the CRA cannot reinsert into your file a disputed item unless the information source verifies its accuracy and completeness. In addition, the CRA must give you a written notice telling you it has reinserted the item. The notice must include the name, address and phone number of the infor- mation source.

- **You can dispute inaccurate items with the source of the information.** If you tell anyone — such as a creditor who reports to a CRA — that you dispute an item, they may not then report the information to a CRA without including a notice of your dispute. In addition, once you've notified the source of the error in writing, it may not continue to report the information if it is, in fact, an error.

- **Outdated information may not be reported.** In most cases, a CRA may not report negative information that is more than seven years old; ten years for bankruptcies.

- **Access to your file is limited.** A CRA may provide information about you only to people with a need recognized by the FCRA — usually to consider an application with a creditor, insurer, employer, landlord, or other business.

- **Your consent is required for reports that are provided to employers, or reports that contain medical information.** A CRA may not give out information about you to your employer, or prospective employer, without your written consent. A CRA may not report medical information about you to creditors, insurers, or employers without your permission.

- **You may choose to exclude your name from CRA lists for unsolicited credit and insurance offers.** Creditors and insurers may use file information as the basis for sending you unsolicited offers of credit or insurance. Such offers must include a toll-free phone number for you to call if you want your name and address removed from future lists. If you call, you must be kept off the lists for two years. If you request, complete, and return the CRA form provided for this purpose, you must be taken off the lists indefinitely.

- **You may seek damages from violators.** If a CRA, a user or (in some cases) a provider of CRA data, violates the FCRA, you may sue them in state or federal court.

The FCRA gives several different federal agencies authority to enforce the FCRA:

FOR QUESTIONS OR CONCERNS REGARDING
PLEASE CONTAC T

CRAs, creditors and others not listed below
Federal Trade Commission
Consumer Response Center- FCRA
Washington, DC 20580 * 202-326-3761

National banks, federal branches/agencies of foreign banks (word "National" or initials "N.A." appear in or after bank's name)
Office of the Comptroller of the Currency
Compliance Management, Mail Stop 6-6
Washington, DC 20219 * 800-613-6743

Federal Reserve System member banks (except national banks, and federal branches/agencies of foreign banks)
Federal Reserve Board
Division of Consumer & Community Affairs
Washington, DC 20551 * 202-452-3693

Savings associations and federally chartered savings banks (word "Federal" or initials "F.S.B." appear in federal institution's name)
Office of Thrift Supervision
Consumer Programs
Washington D.C. 20552* 800- 842-6929

Federal credit unions (words "Federal Credit Union" appear in institution's name)
National Credit Union Administration
1775 Duke Street
Alexandria, VA 22314 * 703-518-6360

State-chartered banks that are not members of the Federal Reserve System
Federal Deposit Insurance Corporation
Division of Compliance & Consumer Affairs
Washington, DC 20429 * 800-934-FDIC

Air, surface, or rail common carriers regulated by former Civil Aeronautics Board or Interstate Commerce Commission
Department of Transportation
Office of Financial Management
Washington, DC 20590 * 202-366-1306

Activities subject to the Packers and Stockyards Act, 1921
Department of Agriculture
Office of Deputy Administrator-GIPSA
Washington, DC 20250 * 202-720-7051

# Fair Credit Reporting

If you've ever applied for a charge account, a personal loan, insurance, or a job, there's a file about you. This file contains information on where you work and live, how you pay your bills, and whether you've been sued, arrested, or filed for bankruptcy.

Companies that gather and sell this information are called Consumer Reporting Agencies (CRAs). The most common type of CRA is the credit bureau. The information CRAs sell about you to creditors, employers, insurers, and other businesses is called a consumer report.

The Fair Credit Reporting Act (FCRA), enforced by the Federal Trade Commission, is designed to promote accuracy and ensure the privacy of the information used in consumer reports. Recent amendments to the Act expand your rights and place additional requirements on CRAs. Businesses that supply information about you to CRAs and those that use consumer reports also have new responsibilities under the law.

Here are some questions consumers commonly ask about consumer reports and CRAs — and the answers. Note that you may have additional rights under state laws. Contact your state Attorney General or local consumer protection agency for more information.

Q. How do I find the CRA that has my report?

A. Contact the CRAs listed in the Yellow Pages under "credit" or "credit rating and reporting." Because more than one CRA may have a file on you, call each until you locate all the agencies maintaining your file. The three major national credit bureaus are:

Equifax, P.O. Box 740241, Atlanta, GA 30374-0241; (800) 685-1111.

Experian (formerly TRW), P.O. Box 2104, Allen, TX 75013; (888) EXPERIAN (397-3742).

Trans Union, P.O. Box 1000, Chester, PA 19022; (800) 916-8800.

* Note: These agencies frequently change their phone numbers and addresses. Please verify before sending personal info in the mail. In addition, anyone who takes action against you in response to a report supplied by a CRA — such as denying your application for credit, insurance, or employment — must give you the name, address, and telephone number of the CRA that provided the report.

Q. Do I have a right to know what's in my report?

A. Yes, if you ask for it. The CRA must tell you everything in your report, including medical information, and in most cases, the sources of the information. The CRA also must give you a list of everyone who has requested your report within the past year — two years for employment related requests.

Q. Is there a charge for my report?

A. Sometimes. There's no charge if a company takes adverse action against you, such as denying your application for credit, insurance or employment, and you request your report within 60 days of receiving the notice of the action. The notice will give you the name, address, and phone number of the CRA. In addition, you're entitled to one free report a year (1) you're unemployed and plan to look for a job within 60 days, (2) you're on welfare, or (3) your report is inaccurate because of fraud. Otherwise, a CRA may charge you up to $9 for a copy of your report.

Q. What can I do about inaccurate or incomplete information?

A. Under the new law, both the CRA and the information provider have responsibilities for correcting inaccurate or incomplete information in your report. To protect all your rights under this law, contact both the CRA and the information provider.

First, tell the CRA in writing what information you believe is inaccurate. CRAs must reinvestigate the items in question - usually within 30 days — unless they consider your dispute frivolous. They also must forward all relevant data you provide about the dispute to the information provider. After the information provider receives notice of a dispute from the CRA, it must investigate, review all relevant information provided by the CRA, and report the results to the CRA. If the information provider finds the disputed information to be inaccurate, it must notify all nationwide CRAs so that they can correct this information in your file.

When the reinvestigation is complete, the CRA must give you the written results and a free copy of your report if the dispute results in a change. If an item is changed or removed, the CRA cannot put the disputed information back in your file unless the information provider verifies its accuracy and completeness, and the CRA gives you a written notice that includes the name, address, and phone number of the provider.

Second, tell the creditor or other information provider in writing that you dispute an item. Many providers specify an address for disputes. If the provider then reports the item to any CRA, it must include a notice of your dispute. In addition, if you are correct — that is, if the information is inaccurate — the information provider may not use it again.

Q. What can I do if the CRA or information provider won't correct the information I dispute?

A. A reinvestigation may not resolve your dispute with the CRA. If that's the case, ask the CRA to include your statement of the dispute in your file and in future reports. If you request, the CRA also will provide your statement to anyone who received a copy of the old report in the recent past. There usually is a fee for this service.

If you tell the information provider that you dispute an item, a notice of your dispute must be included anytime the information provider reports the item to a CRA.

Q. Can my employer get my report?

A. Only if you say it's okay. A CRA may not supply information about you to your employer, or to a prospective employer, without your consent.

Q. Can creditors, employers, or insurers get a report that contains medical information about me?

A. Not without your approval.

Q. What should I know about "investigative consumer reports"?

A. "Investigative consumer reports" are detailed reports that involve interviews with your neighbors or acquaintances about your lifestyle, character, and reputation. They may be used in connection with insurance and employment applications. You'll be notified in writing when a company orders such a report. The notice will explain your right to request certain information about the report from the company you applied to. If your application is rejected, you may get additional information from the CRA. However, the CRA does not have to reveal the sources of the information.

Q. How long can a CRA report negative information?

A. Seven years. There are certain exceptions:

> Information about criminal convictions may be reported without any time limitation.

> Bankruptcy information may be reported for 10 years.

> Information reported in response to an application for a job with a salary of more than $75,000 has no time limit.

> Information reported because of an application for more than $150,000 worth of credit or life insurance has no time limit.

> Information about a lawsuit or an unpaid judgment against you can be reported for seven years or until the statute of limitations runs out, whichever is longer.

Q. Can anyone get a copy of my report?

A. No. Only people with a legitimate business need, as recognized by the FCRA. For example, a company is allowed to get your report if you apply for credit, insurance, employment, or to rent an apartment.

Q. How can I stop a CRA from including me on lists for unsolicited credit and insurance offers?

A. Creditors and insurers may use CRA file information as a basis for sending you unsolicited offers. These offers must include a toll-free number for you to call if you want to remove your name and address from lists for two years; completing a form that the CRA provides for this purpose will keep your name off the lists permanently.

Q. Do I have the right to sue for damages?

A. You may sue a CRA, a user or — in some cases — a provider of CRA data, in state or federal court for most violations of the FCRA. If you win, the defendant will have to pay damages and reimburse you for attorney fees to the extent ordered by the court.

Q. Are there other laws I should know about?

A. Yes. If your credit application was denied, the Equal Credit Opportunity Act requires creditors to specify why — if you ask. For example, the creditor must tell you whether you were denied because you have "no credit file" with a CRA or because the CRA says you have "delinquent obligations." The ECOA also requires creditors to consider additional information you might supply about your credit history. You may want to find out why the creditor denied your application before you contact the CRA.

Q. Where should I report violations of the law?

A. Although the FTC can't act as your lawyer in private disputes, information about your experiences and concerns is vital to the enforcement of the Fair Credit Reporting Act. Send your questions or complaints to: Consumer Response Center – FCRA, Federal Trade Commission, Washington, D.C. 20580.

# INDEX

www.ingramcontent.com/pod-product-compliance
Lightning Source LLC
Chambersburg PA
CBHW062043090426
42740CB00016B/3003